THE EVOLUTION OF JAPAN AND OTHER PAPERS

THE EVOLUTION OF JAPAN AND OTHER PAPERS

LALA LAJPAT RAI

GYAN

Published by

Gyan Publishing House
5, Ansari Road
Daryaganj, New Delhi-110002
Phone: 011-47034999, 9811692060
E-mail: books@gyanbooks.com

Distribution Network
gyanbooks.com
India, USA, Canada, UK, Australia

ISBN: 978-93-7133-350-4 (PB)

First Published,

2nd Impression 2025

Printed at: Gyan Press, Delhi.

THE EVOLUTION OF JAPAN AND OTHER PAPERS
Author Lala Lajpat Rai

The Evolution of Japan and Other Papers

BY

LAJPAT RAI.

R. CHATTERJEE
MODERN REVIEW OFFICE
210-3-1, Cornwallis Street, Calcutta.

The Evolution of Japan and Other Papers

THE EVOLUTION OF JAPAN

I

THE Anglo-Indian and British critics of Indian nationalists are very fond of charging the latter with impatience and of pointing out to them, day in and day out that Rome was not built in a day; that most of their troubles are due to a want of initiative on the part of the Indians themselves; that representative and democratic institutions are foreign to the genius of the Eastern people; and that it is unreasonable for them to demand what the British have built up after centuries of effort and struggle. We are also very often told that institutions grow from below and can neither be imposed from above nor grafted from without. Many of these statements are at best half-truths, and fallacious. Some are absolutely stupid. This is proved by a study of the growth of institutions in the new world, but even more forcibly is this demonstrated by the development of Japan and the revolution in China. China is not yet on her legs, although the Chinese Government and the Chinese people are working hard to make up for lost time. Over 3,000 Chinese students in receipt of Government scholarships are always studying in the Colleges and Universities of the U. S. A. Every year a batch of them returns to the country and takes up important positions therein and engages in the work of developing China. A fresh batch is then sent to take the places vacated by those that have returned.

The number of Chinese scholars in receipt of Government scholarships, in the Colleges and Universities of the U. S. A., is thus constantly on the increase. Every year the number sent up comes to hundreds. Add to this the number that are receiving education at their own expense in America, England, Germany and Japan. In Japan alone the number of Chinese students receiving education in Japanese higher institutions, Colleges, and Technical Schools and Technological Institutes exceeds 5,000. China has decided to introduce conscription from the beginning of the next year and if she can keep herself floating for a few years more, she may yet startle the world with her formidable strength, regained, rejuvenated and refreshed. Her resources are simply inexhaustible and her people perhaps the most intelligent and hard-working and industrious in the whole world. China, however, is yet in the early stages of her new life. Japan, on the other hand, is quite grown. She has reached a stage in her evolution which entitles her to a place in the list of world powers. It cannot be said that she has reached the zenith of her possibilities, but her progress has, so far, been sufficiently marked and pronounced to justify our saying that she has falsified the croakings of her western critics and their dictum that Western wine could not be put into Eastern bottles. Japan is a splendid example of what can be achieved by a nation guided by a benevolent national Government devoted to her people.

Any one seeing Japan as she is or reading of her from a distance is liable to forget the most important fact that she was almost nothing in the sixties of the 19th century. The modern regime in Japan began from after 1868 A. D. At that time Japan was still living her secluded primitive life; her people, in spite of the smallness of their numbers, were divided into numerous classes, sects and even castes and sub-castes. The Administration was carried on on primitive lines and the population was oppressed by a large number of feudal lords who exercised more or less independent powers in their fiefs. The Government was a despotic military autocracy. The sovereign had no voice in the affairs of the state, which were in his name administered by the military chief of the nation. The people were steeped in dense ignorance and overridden by superstition. The country had a civilization of its own kind, with its religion and arts imported from China and India, but there was nothing like system or order in the life of the nation. Judged by Western standards it was all chaos and disorder and even barbarism. Intercourse with civilisation was confined to the exchange of a few commodities of everyday use. The imports by far exceeded the exports. The only articles of export were some silk goods or curiosities of art. All foreign trade, whatever it was, was in the hands of a few Dutch shippers and a few Spaniards who had the monopoly of it by Royal grants. Japan was not open to the civilized world and the latter knew almost nothing about it. No foreigners were allowed in the country except the few traders referred to above and foreign trade was absolutely forbidden to the sons of the soil. Japan was as if a closed cell which kept its doors shut and had even no windows or ventilators for light or air from without. The world knew almost nothing about her, nor did she know anything about the world. She was a self-contained country in every sense of the word, without any ambition to enter the comity of nations, which she was forced to do at the point of the bayonet. Her aristocrats were happy and contented in their mutual quarrels, jealousies and competition. The people existed only to toil and labour for their lords, living on simple food and simple clothing, reserving the rest for their feudal lords. It requires some imagination to believe that within less than fifty years (from 1868 to 1910) Japan should have won the position which she now occupies in the world. Large numbers of Japanese are now permanently settled in America (North and South), in the Hawaii islands, in the Phillippines, in the Malay Archipelago in China, Manchuria and Mongolia, possessing vast property and carrying on agricultural, industrial and commercial operations on a gigantic scale. There is hardly a country on the face of the globe where the little Jap is not to be found, holding his head erect, proud of his position by virtue of his strength at home, conscious of the great part he is playing on the world stage and striving for even greater and nobler achievements. At home Japan has a first class Army and a great Navy, built by the Sovereign with the willing aid and co-operation of her people. But what is still more remarkable is the successful introduction and working of representative democratic institutions; a Parliamentary form of Government and an up-to-date system of education. Within 50 years Japan has grown into a teacher of the Orient and a supplier of all the necessaries and luxuries of life which the latter used to get from the Occident. Japan has not yet reached the height of her possibilities either in the form of her Government or in the development of her resources or in general progress, but what she has achieved within the last 50 years is monumental and wonderful. She is an object-lesson to those who deprecate the granting of constitutions by sovereigns without agitation, without pressure from the people. She is an example and a successful example of how a Government can educate a people in democratic methods by the grant of democratic institutions. Modern Japan was hardly out of her teens when her monarch decided to give her a constitution and granted her Parliamentary Government. Modern education in Japan was not more than 20 years old when the Japanese, who did not before know what was liberty of thought and liberty of speech in the modern sense of these terms, began to enjoy both. Reading the translations from the Japanese papers which are a regular feature of the daily papers published in English in the country, one sees no difference, so far as the liberty of speech and press and thought are concerned, between the Japanese Press on the one hand and the English and the American Press on the other. Japan is about to enter on the last stage of Parliamentary Government, viz., Government by parties. The affairs of the Empire are administered by a cabinet without any interference by the sovereign.

Japan is a singular example of a democracy being trained by responsibility and trust. It was not a case of first deserve and then desire. It was a case of a father showing his entire confidence in his child and handing him over the reins before he had proved his fitness by the standards set up by Western nations. No education is so effective as that afforded by a position of responsibility. The wonderful development of Japan is due to the wise and tactful management and guidance of the Japanese people by their Government. Every kind of help has been ungrudgingly and unreservedly given to enable the people to develop and cultivate a democratic spirit, to develop their resources, their trade and their industries. If Japan had chosen to proceed by the inductive method, it would have taken her centuries to achieve what she has gained within fifty years, and in the meantime there was every likelihood of her being devoured by sharks always on the look-out for victims. Japan has been saved by the trust placed by her monarch in her people and by the ungrudging help given by her Government in initiating all measures that were necessary for her education and development. With these introductory remarks I propose to sketch out for the benefit of my readers an account of the development of industries and trade in Japan.

II

The factors which contribute to the Industrial and Commercial progress of a nation are the following :

(*a*) Capital.

(*b*) Skilled and unskilled labour.

(*c*) Spirit of enterprise and co-operation.

(*d*) Field for the distribution of products on reasonable price, and protection from unfair competition.

(*e*) Facilities of communication.

(*f*) Capacity to organise.

I propose to take each of the heads separately and state what was done by the Japanese Government to create these factors. I will show that under each head and in each case the initiative came from the Government and the Government bore almost all the initial losses and expenses in connection therewith. It should be kept in mind that for 25 years or more of these 50 years Japan laboured in face of international treaties which denied her freedom of action in regulating her tariff. During this time the foreigners in Japan enjoyed full extraterritorial jurisdiction and thus lorded over both the Government and the people.

III

The organisation and the supply of Capital.

I have already said that Modern Japan dates from 1868 A. D. It was in that year that the monarchy was restored to its proper position and the country united under one Government. Such financial houses as existed before that date were not bankers in the modern sense of the term and there was absolutely nothing which could be said to resemble joint-stock enterprise. In the whole country there were only three financial houses which could be called bankers even in the old sense. International commerce was prohibited and even the domestic trade was not quite free, on account of clash of interests which resulted from a multiplicity of authorities. Merchants and artizans were despised and the only classes that were respected were the *Samurai* (members of military clans equivalent to Indian Rajputs) and farmers. The three houses that engaged in financial business represented three families or clans, and their business consisted "in receiving the tax moneys, paying them to the Government in drafts, financing the barons, exchanging gold, silver and copper," and doing such other banking business as was required in those days. They were really Government treasures and never undertook the functions of a bank in the circulation of money by lending and discounting. There was not a single Japanese in the country at that time who knew anything of Modern Banking or of the western methods of business. The first step taken by the Government was the organising of the "*Shohoshe*" (Business Bureau) in 1868, followed in the next year by the establishment of the *Ysushoshi* (viz., the Commercial Bureau). The Business Bureau "was intended to take charge of national revenues to *encourage industry and to promote trade and production by lending money at low rates of interest*"; "the Commercial Bureau had for its objects the development of home and foreign trade and the increase of Government income. Under its control Commercial Companies were established to engage in home and foreign trade, and Exchange Companies were organised to assist the Commercial Companies and also to facilitate the general circulation of money. Three exchange companies were formed by wealthy merchants under the Government's advice and insistence" (Fifty Years of Japan, by Count Okuma, p. 487).

Baron Shibusawa, the writer of the chapter on the development of banking in Count Okuma's book (Fifty Years of Japan), adds that "the Government did much towards protecting and encouraging them by lending them capital and by granting them special privilege to issue"........gold and silver notes "against certain reserve funds required to be set aside." It may be stated in passing that Baron Shibusawa, who has been the President of the First Bank ever since its foundation in 1873 A.D., does not know a word of English. In one of his visits to Paris long ago, he had picked up a few French words, but he speaks and writes only Japanese and transacts his business principally in Japanese with the help of English-knowing Japanese as Secretaries. Most of the pioneers of modern Japan are in the same position so far as the knowledge of the modern languages is concerned, the premier Count Okuma being one of them.

The exchange companies formed in 1869 worked only for four years. "Lacking proper men of ability to manage their affairs they went from bad to worse, for their expenses exceeded their income and they incurred a considerable amount of debt." We are told that "in spite of all the protection given and the special privileges granted by the Government ....their object failed, yet the benefits conferred by their creation were immense, for they introduced into society the principle of a joint-stock company, set an example, and gained experience."

In 1870 Prince Ito was deputed to America to observe and study financial institutions and their working. As a result of his studies the Government floated a scheme for the establishment of National Banks, the first of which was opened in 1873. The banks were opened with Government help and under Government Regulations. We are told by Baron Shibusawa that "the bankers of that time had little or no experience in banking business and did not know the necessity of paying careful attention to the balance of foreign trade with a view to regulating the amount of notes issued" by them. Other circumstances (among them the bankruptcy of the leading merchants) also contributed to the prostration of the Government scheme and in the course of four years from 1872 to 1876 only four banks came into existence. Therefore in August 1876 new Regulations for national Banks were promulgated, which facilitated the opening of new Banks. The majority of these Banks had national bonds as capital and only one quarter of them had their capital in currency. In three years from 1876 to June 1879, 148 new banks came into existence with an aggregate capital of about 40 million yen, of which 29 million yen was in bonds. This rapid increase in the number of banks on the strength of Government bonds and with power to issue notes, etc., again led to disaster. There was constant fluctuation in the price of commodities; while the prices of commodities were going up, the bankers found their business active and many of them increased their capital; but when the reaction set in, "business was depressed, enterprises were suspended, factories were in decay.........and merchants and manufacturers became bankrupt." The Government, then, limited the number of national banks and promulgated regulations for the establishment of private banks. The first private bank was established in 1876 and for three or four years it remained the only private bank. By 1880 the number of private banks had risen to 317, and by 1883 to 896.

In 1879 the Government organised the Yokohama Specie Bank with a view to afford facilities to Japanese to engage in foreign trade. One-third of the capital was subscribed by Government, "who gave it encouragement and protection in various forms and ways." At that time there was a scarcity of silver in the country and 100 yen in silver could purchase 170 yen in notes. The result was that 1,400,000 yen in silver were paid by Government against 400,000 yen in silver by the general subscribers and 1,600,000 yen were accepted in notes. In 1882, *i.e.*, within 2 years of its starting its business, the Bank found itself in such difficulties that some of the shareholders proposed closing the business. Violent disputes arose, but the Government intervened and bought out the dissenting shareholders. Meanwhile the estimated losses of the Bank had reached the colossal figure of over a million yen (*i.e.*, about ¼th of its capital was gone). The Government again extended its help and saved the situation. This bank is now one of the premier banks of Japan and has rendered inestimable services in the development of the foreign trade of Japan.

The present position of the bank may be judged from the following figures :

Authorised Capital	...	48,000,000	Yen.
Paid up ...	...	30,000,000	do.
Reserve Fund	...	19,600,000	do.

It has branches in all the big countries of the world including India. With rapid increase in the number of banks, national and private, the necessity of a central institution to regulate the circulation of monev was felt and in 1882 the Bank of Japan was organised with the following objects : First, to be "a central bank whereof all the banks in the country should be regarded as branches which should open mutual correspondence, cultivate the spirit of co-operation and secure the easy circulation of money throughout the land; secondly, to lend capital to other banks at a moderate rate of interest, thus helping to raise their credit and develop their business; thirdly, to engage specially in discounting bills, to quicken the movement of capital, to keep money easy and to lower the rate of interest; fourthly, to take charge of the receipt and issue of Government moneys and to utilise these moneys in discounting bills, etc., when there was any surplus; and lastly, to control the collection and distribution of gold by raising and lowering the rate of discount, and, when necessary, to attract gold from abroad.

On the establishment of the Bank of Japan, the original National Banks were converted into private banks. A few were dissolved. Thus within less than 20 years of the Restoration (1868) Japan developed a system of National Banking which now competes on almost equal terms with foreign banking and which is the stable rock on which its industrial and commercial prosperity stands.

The course of this development was by no means smooth and easy. Many difficulties were encountered and there were several disasters. But in the end by the benevolent guidance and help of Government and the co-operation of the people and the Government all troubles were overcome, with the happiest possible results to the trade and industry of the country. There are many skeletons and carcasses buried under the edifice, but the edifice is all the more strong and vigorous for that fact. Failures, ending in successes, add to the glory and the triumph of the latter and to the pleasure and pride of those who contributed towards the realisation of the final goal by sacrificing all in pioneer work. Yet this was only possible under the initiative and guidance and with the assistance and never-failing and timely help of the National Government.

But we have not yet finished with the story of Banking in Modern Japan. We propose to give two instances of how the Japanese Government helped the country in financial crises. The first occurred immediately after the war with China in April and May 1898. It is stated that the rate of interest became abnormally high; many of the companies found it very difficult to collect their subscribed capital and were compelled to dissolve. It was feared that a panic would ensue. The Government at once came to the rescue. The Finance Department used a portion of the Chinese indemnity in taking over the debentures of the Industrial Bank to the extent of 3,740,000 yen and ordered the bank to give financial assistance to companies having good prospects. Within six months the situation was saved.

In 1900 again the country was facing a serious financial set-back. From December 1900 to February 1901 some banks had to suspend payment; and other banks suffered losses. In April the money market in Osaka (the chief manufacturing centre of Japan) fell into a state of alarm and several banks had to suspend payment. In May again, the banks had losses of a violent nature. During the depression sales of goods were obstructed, and merchants and manufacturers found themselves in straits. Even good banks suffered on account of delay in collecting their loans, and fall in the prices of their securities and small demand for capital. The Bank of Japan and other influential banks, however, stepped in and saved the situation.

Banks with Special Privilege.

Besides the banks doing general business the Japanese Government has established a number of special banks with special privilege for the protection and promotion of agriculture and industries. In August 1897 the Hypothec Bank and during 1897 to 1900 forty-six Agricultural and Industrial banks were established, one in each Prefecture. These two kinds of banks have for their main object the lending of money for long periods at low interest against the security of landed estates, the money being refunded by yearly instalments, and the encouragement of the progress and development of agriculture and industry.

The Hypothec Bank has the special privilege of issuing premium-bearing bonds to the amount of ten times its paid-up capital and it receives a subsidy for ten years from the Government so as to make good any shortage in declaring a dividend of 5 per cent. per annum on its capital.

The Agricultural and Industrial banks enjoy the privilege of issuing debentures to the amount of five times their paid-up capital. The Government, through the Prefectural offices subscribed 10 millions yen towards the capital of these banks. Of the shares thus subscribed, the banks were exempted from paying dividends for the first fifteen years, being further permitted to carry to their reserve funds the dividends earned in the succeeding five years.

Similarly in 1899 the Government enacted the law of the Hokkaido Colonization Bank. Hokkaido is the name of the Northern group of Japanese islands which are sparsely populated and not properly developed. The object of this bank is to supply capital for the colonization of Hokkaido. The Bank enjoys the privilege of issuing debentures to the extent of five times its paid-up capital. Besides the Government is a shareholder to the amount of 1,000,000 yen and waives the right to receive a dividend for ten years. The bank's nominal capital is 5,000,000. In March 1900 was established the Japan Industrial Bank. Its object is solely to supply money on the security of national and local bonds, debentures and shares in companies, subscribing for these bonds, debentures and shares; engaging in trust business; discounting guaranteed bills; and making loans to financial corporations as established by law. Thc bank can issue debentures to the amount of ten times its paid-up capital, and with the sanction of the minister controlling the Bank, it can issue debentures without regard to the limit when there is occasion to supply money to enterprises of public interest in foreign countries. If the bank is unable to declare a dividend of 5 per cent., the Government grants a subsidy sufficient to make good the shortage for five years. The authorised capital of the bank is 17,500,000 yen.

My object in giving the above sketch of the

development of modern banking in Japan is to show to my countrymen,

(1) that they need not and should not be discouraged by failures;

(2) that they need not and should not copy the methods of foreign banking in all its details; they should adopt their salient features working out the details as suits the requirements of Indian conditions;

(3) that they should not discard the advice and co-operation of such of their countrymen as do not know English. In this matter the Indian banks suffer from the necessity of transacting their business in English from which the Japanese banks are free.

In giving this account, I do not pronounce on the soundness or otherwise of the methods and principles followed by the Japanese in organising their banks, but so much is clear that Japan owes its present industrial and commercial prosperity to the foresight, sagacity and patriotism of her Government and that but for Government initiative, help and guidance Japan might have been perhaps as backward in its industries as India is. This should open the eyes of such of our critics as take pleasure in running us down with charges of lack of initiative and lack of enterprise. We are told in season and out of season that we depend too much on Government and that Government cannot legitimately help us in starting new industries and in subsidising and protecting them against foreign competition. Our captains of industries and pioneers have had to work single-handed, against odds and formidable rivals. That there have been failures on account of incompetency, inexperience and sometimes even dishonesty is true, but the wonder is not that there have been so many failures but that under the circumstances we should have even attained the measure of success we have. The Government of the country, which should have helped materially in the development of purely Indian banking, have stood aloof and have observed a neutrality which has sometimes added a point to other difficulties and hastened or expedited the disaster. Yet we have to go on and my countrymen should not lose heart by failures. These temporary lapses should not bring us to a standstill, but should goad us to better and even more determined efforts to organise capital for the development of our industries and for the progress of our trade. We may as well press the Government to help us but we should never relax our own efforts to build up our banking, as sound and stable banking alone can furnish the basis of industrial and commercial regeneration.

What the Government of Japan has done in other respects will follow in other articles.

Industries.

Forty-five years ago the industrial situation in Japan was very similar to what India faced in the early days of British rule. Before the advent of western influences both the countries were, so to say, industrially self-contained and supplied the needs of their people by their own manufactures. The difference was this that in India there was no embargo on the importation of foreign goods, no restraints imposed by Government on the choice of industrial pursuits and no prohibition of foreign travel or trade with foreigners, as in Japan. Before 1868, the Japanese people were not free to choose their industrial pursuits; all industries and crafts were more or less hereditary and divided into guilds or unions; every one was bound by law to undergo apprenticeship for a certain number of years before he could set up a business for himself; no one outside a guild or union could start an industry or business of his own. Besides, the country was not open to foreigners. A few Dutch and Spaniards were allowed certain trading privileges by special permission of the ruling authorities. Nor were the sons of the soil free to go out and travel in or trade with foreign countries. What happened may best be described in the words of one of the greatest living authorities on the subject, Count Okuma, the ex-premier of Japan. In writing an introduction to a publication called "Japan's Industries" he remarks :

"Since the Restoration and in consequence of it, Japanese industry has undergone a great change both in regard to its nature and its extent. When, by force of circumstances, Japan was compelled to open her ports and enter into treaty obligations with foreign powers, her import duty was prescribed by the terms of the various treaties at the low average rate of 5 per cent *ad valorem*...... Japan's adoption of Free Trade was done neither willingly nor voluntarily but at the instance of the Treaty powers. It was this pressure from without which helped to bring about the industrial upheaval ; but the revolution was caused by pressure from within."

The pressure from within was the sudden change in the tastes of the people brought about by a sudden influx of foreign ideas and by contact with nations who held a superior political position in the world. The adoption of the foreign dress for the army led to the civilians also taking to it as an emblem of respectability and superiority. "Those who appeared attired in European clothes," says the Count, "were saluted everywhere, with profound bows." Throughout the whole country there was a general craze for everything European.* There arose, both in those commodities which are the necessaries of life, and in those which are mere luxuries, a demand for things which had hitherto been unknown in the Japanese market. This resulted in a sudden transformation in the character of the nation's industries. Many of the old industries became extinct and numerous competent craftsmen lost their occupation. In the words of the Count,

"The Japanese industrial world was thrown into a state of consternation at this surprising revolution and the majority of the craftsmen were quite at a loss as to how best to adapt themselves to their new

* There has taken place a great change in the sentiments of the people, in this respect, since then. A reaction is now in full swing.

surroundings." "........The Japanese Government, being deprived by the treaties of her tariff autonomy, was unable to obtain revenue by a protective† system. And there were no other means by which native industries could be protected. The people had neither the knowledge nor the ability to utilise machinery nor to create new industries by the investment of capital."

The result was that "the country was flooded with goods of foreign manufacture, and Japan which for centuries had remained a self-supporting country, thus found herself forced to depend upon foreign manufacturers," even "for her daily wants and needs," not to speak of "luxuries and articles of toilet, etc." Up till 1908 her imports exceeded the exports. In 1898 her imports exceeded the exports by 112 millions of yen. In 1900 by 82 million yen. In 1905 the figure rose to 167 million till it fell to 58 million in 1908. It was under these circumstances that the Japanese Government set about to take actual steps to protect her old arts and crafts, as well as to introduce the European industries into Japan, with such wonderful results.

† There is a rigid protective tariff now, of which we shall speak in another article.

She is now a formidable rival to such manufacturing countries as Great Britain, Germany and the United States of America.

In a few paragraphs we propose to state what those steps were. Firstly, active and energetic measures were taken to inform the world of the ancient art products of Japan and of her exquisite workmanship. Within four years of the Restoration, the Government of Japan took steps to participate in the Great International Exhibition held at Vienna in 1873. A special Bureau was created to collect exhibits and do everything necessary in connection with the exhibition. Count Okuma (ex-Premier of Japan) was appointed president and a Senator as Vice-President. A special official mission consisting of seventy Government officials was sent to the Exhibition to push on the sale of Japan art products, and a large number of artizans were deputed to study European tastes, as well as to make themselves acquainted with the condition of modern industries. After the exhibition some of the most able among the members of the mission were despatched to different European countries to study the various scientific subjects bearing on industry. In the year following the Vice-President returned to Japan, with samples of European piecegoods, knitted work, raw materials for dyeing and weaving and tools and machines. All these were shown to the people interested in them in the country.

(2) Again when the International Exposition for the centenary commemoration of American Independence was held at Philadelphia, the Japan Government took part "in the hope of making known to the nations of the world Japanese arts and manufactures." The advantages thus derived were manifold; for while on the one hand, the exhibition helped to introduce the latest and the most improved appliances used in western countries into Japan, on the other, with the wide spread of technical education in Japan new industries hitherto unknown there were established. A nation alive to the importance of her industries and in a position to protect her old industries and start new ones, always benefits by participating in international expositions and by organising national exhibitions. On the contrary, a nation powerless in these respects suffers thereby. The living nations and the powerful industrial and manufacturing organisations of other countries take away the samples

of articles in demand in the country and flood the latter with the cheap imitation of the same, to the ruin of the local and national craftsman. That was done by Germany by flooding India with cheap imitation shawls, phulkarees, rugs, images, etc., etc. Japan on the other hand benefited by these exhibitions. Industrial and commercial exhibitions are now an enduring feature of the national life of Japan. She never misses an opportunity of participating in international expositions also. In order to create a demand for Japanese art products and goods, the Japanese Government even established a subsidised business in Tokyo in 1874 by the name of "Keiya Kosho Kaisha" with the special object of exporting Japanese works of art to foreign countries. It is said that this company engaged in business with great energy and materially helped to advertise Japanese gold lacquer wares, metal works, textile fabrics, and ceramic products, in western markets. The direct result of this is the rejuvenating of old Japanese industries which had declined in the early years of the Meiji period.

(3) Of the steps which the Imperial Government of Japan took to introduce and encourage new

industries, the first and one of the most important was the establishment of model factories at considerable expense, where experience was gained in new manufactures at the expense of the State. Some of the concerns started by the Government for purposes of example and experience were then sold to private companies. Samples were brought from foreign countries and circulated among industrial circles at Government expense. At first these concerns were placed in charge of European experts, but they were replaced by Japanese as soon as some were found to take their place.

(4) The Imperial Household established in 1890 the Institution of Imperial Artists with the object of encouraging the arts of Japan. Experts of skill and merit were honored by Imperial mandate, thus encouraging others to follow in their foot-steps.

(5) The Department of Education also organised an Academy of Fine Arts in which both the theory and practise of painting, sculpture, lacquer work and modelling were and are taught.

(6) But what was most important, was the ample provision made for technical education. Numberless scholars were sent abroad to the different countries of

Europe and to America at Government expense, and schools and colleges were established at home to produce experts and skilled workmen.

The number of students of both sexes which Japan has sent to Europe and America since the opening of the country to foreign intercourse must reach "enormous figures," specially when students who have gone abroad at their own expense are included. But what the Japanese Government is still doing in the matter may be gathered from the following figures.

At the end of the year 1905-6, the Japanese Government was maintaining 86 scholars in Europe and America. The figures for the succeeding years are as follows :—

1906-7	85	1909-10	130
1907-8	98	1910-11	124
1908-9	113	1911-12	123
		1912-13	132

It might be noted that the number has been increasing. Let us now see what provision the Japanese Government has made at home for producing experts and skilled workmen.

The following figures show the aid which the

Japanese Government has given to low-grade Agricultural, Fishery, Commercial, Navigation, Technical and similar schools. In 1907-08 there were 318 such schools in receipt of a total grant of 321,880 yen,

1908-09	320 Schools.	323,830 Yen.
1909-10	328 ,,	324,480 ,,
1910-11	371 ,,	336,150 ,,
1911-12	385 ,,	337,730 ,,

Besides the Government maintained (in 1913) 5 Higher Commercial Schools at a cost of from 64,711 yen per year to 117,158 yen per year. In these higher Commercial Schools provision is made for instruction in all the important languages of the world.

Besides, the Government maintains 6 Higher Technical Schools at a cost varying from 71,314 yen per year to 167,384 yen per year, one Mining School at a cost of 77,219 yen per year, 2 Higher Agricultural Schools, 3 Higher Sericultural Schools, one Foreign Language School and one Fishery Institute.

In the Higher Technical Schools the number of instructors is 175 and that of students 2781.

In the Higher Technical School the number of instructors (in five of them only, the figures for the 6th not being available) is 216 and the number of students 2,624. In the Foreign Language School there are 36 instructors and 674 students.

When reading these figures, the readers should always remember the size of the country and its population.

The number of students who have graduated from these schools within the last 40 years will reach to enormous figures. It is they who have so materially contributed to the industrial development of Japan. In one of the small glass factories, at Tokyo, visited by me, the expert in charge was receiving only 50 yen a month and the other labourers were in receipt of 20 to 80 cents each daily (*i.e.* from 5 As. to 20 As.). These latter included the blowers and the moulders, etc. In a leather tanning factory working with a capital of 500,000 yen, the expert in charge, who has completed his education in America, is in receipt of 130 yen a month, while a graduate of the Higher Technical School of Tokyo was getting only 30 yen a month. These figures give an idea of how cheap skilled knowledge in Japan is. The reason is the plentiful supply of it every year from technical schools.

As for unskilled labour it is as cheap as, if not

even cheaper than, in India. A domestic servant in Tokyo can be had from 3 yen a month if female and for 4 yen if a male. The following figures taken from the Japan Year Book (1915) will give an idea of the conditions of skilled and unskilled labour in Japan.

		Wages per week in Yen.
Brick-layer	...	7·07
Carpenter	...	5·60
Painter	...	3·26
Smith	...	4·69
Compositor	...	3·57

The average daily wages of such artizans and craftsmen as tailors, shoe-makers, confectioners, tobacco-cutters, carpenters, plasterers, stone-cutters, sawyers, tile-roofers, brick-layers, ship-builders, cabinet-makers, cart-makers, harness-makers, lacquerers, jewellers, blacksmiths, potters, silk-spinners, gardeners, fishermen, farm labourers, paper-makers, plumbers, ranged in 1906 from 21 cents in the case of a female weaver to 82 cents in the case of a bricklayer. In the majority of these cases the wages were below

60 cents a day. Since 1906 there has been some rise in the wages, but hardly worth considering. In the tables given in the Year Book the average daily wages of an ordinary day labourer are fixed at 58 cents but from actual enquiries in the different factories I learnt that a good many labourers received only 20 cents a day. A Cent of Japanese money is equivalent to a *paisa* of Indian money, perhaps a little less. A Yen is equal to 1 ¼ Rupee.

This cheap labour would not have benefited Japan at all, but for the plentiful supply of skilled labour and a protective tariff, both of which owe their initiative and development to the national policy of the Japanese Government.

III

The third factor which has contributed to the free development of the industries of Japan is her merchant marine. Here again we find that it was the Government of Japan that took the initiative and gave material financial and other support to private enterprise in this line.

At the time of the Restoration in 1868 A.D., Japan had practically no merchant marine. In 1870 the Kaish Kaisha, the first Japanese Steamship Co., established the first regular service between Tokyo and Osaka, two coast-towns, *via* Yokohama and Kobe, also coast-towns, under instructions from Government, the lines leaving thrice a month. In 1875 another company opened the Yokohama Shanghai line and next year extended their service to other ports on the Chinese and Russian coasts. In 1876 Japanese licensed mariners numbered only 76 and of these *only 4 were Japanese subjects*. In that year there was only one Japanese pilot as against 15 of foreign nationality. In 1914 there were 26 Japanese pilots as against 6 foreign. In 1895 there were 4,135 Japanese licensed mariners as against 835 foreigners. Ordinary seamen aggregated 38,217 in 1900 and 202,710 in 1904.

In 1891 the volume of Japan's merchant vessels did not exceed 15,000 tons gross, but by 1896 it had increased to 109,000 tons as a result of the purchase of foreign vessels by the Government. The total tonnage existing at the end of 1903 of 979,000 tons jumped to 1,527,000 tons in 1905. The latest returns at the end of March 1914 represent the gross tonnage of steamers at 1,538,000 and that of sailing ships at 494,000.

In 1896 a legal provision was made for granting bounties to the builders or purchasers of vessels and for subsidising the shipping industry. It was in 1898 that the first large steamer was built in Japanese Dockyards. It was of 6,000 tons. Since then the Japanese Dockyards have built steamers of 10,000 tons displacement and two dreadnaughts of 27,500 tons. At the end of 1912 the private ship-yards numbered 228. The Government has been regularly giving a bounty on every ship since 1896. In 1912 the Japanese shipbuilding companies built 7 ships of 17,183 tons, in 1913, four of 34,478 tons and in 1914 fourteen of 66,329 tons. In May, 1915, the Japanese shipbuilders had in hand orders for 51 vessels of total tonnage of 212,100 tons.

Besides bounties for shipbuilding the Government of Japan has been subsidising regular services. Under the law of 1896 the subsidies were of two kinds; a general subsidy granted on specified routes and another open to all steamers in conformity with the provisions of the law. In 1910 the law was modified abolishing the general subsidy and restricting it to over-sea navigation; for example, (1) The European route, (2) The North American route, (3) The South American route, (4) The Australian route. The latest addition is the Java route.

The vessels to be used in the subsidised navigation must be home-built vessels of over 3,000 tons gross, not less than 15 years old and having a speed exceeding 12 nautical miles per hour. For foreign-built vessels under 5 years old and put on service with the sanction of the authorities one half of the subsidy is granted. For vessels built according to plans approved by competent authorities a specially high subsidy is allowed. 26 steamers of 5,000 to 13,500 gross tonnage with a speed of 13 to 20 knots were engaged in this over-sea subsidised service in June last. Since then the number has risen. Coasting trade in Japan is forbidden to steamers flying foreign flags. Besides, the Government subsidises the coasting and near sea services also liberally. The amount of the latter subsidy alone comes to about 2 million yens.

At the end of December, 1914, the number of Japanese registered steamers reached the total of 1577 with a gross tonnage of 1,577,025 tons.

The five years term of subsidy contracts expired in 1914 and the Government had to renew contracts for one year on its own responsibility, as the bills could not be passed in time owing to the dissolution of the Parliament.

Under the new arrangement sanctioned by Parliament the European service gets a subsidy of 8,657,989 yen in five years beginning with 1,832,806 yen in 1915-16. The North American Service gets 13,855,010 yen, the South American 1,446,888 and the Australian 875,501 yen, which means that in the next five years the Japanese Government will pay a subsidy of about 40 million yen on these four High Sea services alone, equal to 60 million in Indian Rupees.

How the Japanese have eliminated foreigners from their marine will be clear from the following table. We give the figures for 1913 :

	Japanese.	Foreigners.
1st class Captains	1111	179
,, Chief Mates	681	31
,, Second ,,	1253	11
2nd class Captains	702	0

	Japanese	Foreigners.
2nd class Chief Mates	1,489	3
,, Second ,,	3248	1
3rd class Captains	92	0
,, Mates	11424	1
Chief Engineers	1022	79
1st class ,,	1883	43
2nd ,, ,,	1517	2
3rd ,, ,,	3745	2

I do not think readers require it to be explained how national marine helps national industries and national trade. The thing is obvious.

IV

Customs Duties.

Reading Count Okuma's preface to a volume published in 1910 under the name of "Japan Industries" one might think that Japan was a Free Trade country but the following extracts from Count Okuma's Fifty Years of Japan, Volume I, p. 371, show that Japan has never been a Free Trade country.

Marquis Matsugata, the writer of the Chapter on "Japan's Finance" says :

"The customs duties at the time when Japan's door was opened to the world, were fixed on an average, at the rate of 20 per cent. on imports. But as a result of interference on the part of foreign countries during the old *regime*, the actual customs duties both on imports and exports, which the new *regime* inherited from the old, averaged only 5 per cent. This system of 5 per cent. customs duties had been rendered incapable of expansion by the treaties then existing, and therefore could not vary with the varying demands of the Imperial Treasury or with the condition of commerce and industry. In short it had no elasticity."

As a result of new treaties beginning with 1894 and in force since January 1899, duties on imports were fixed at 10 per cent., *ad valorem*, and those on exports were soon afterwards altogether abolished. The statutory tariff rates have since then been revised from time to time. The income from customs dues in 1899 amounted to less than 7 million yen. In 1913 the income was 73,580,000 yen and the average percentage of custom duty was 19.98. The actual scales at which duty is charged on manufactured goods are pretty prohibitive. Even an American writer calls them excessive.

Then there are other kinds of protection which the Japanese Government affords to some branches of the national commerce; for example, no foreigner can acquire the ownership of Japanese ships or even any shares in steamship companies, nor in the Bank of Japan, the Yokohama Specie Bank, or the Agricultural and Industrial Bank. No foreigner can acquire "the right to work mines" or can "become a member of the Stock Exchange" or can "engage in the emigration business." Until recently the ownership of land was prohibited to foreigners, but when the Americans raised the question of Japanese acquiring rights of ownership in lands in California the Japanese Government abolished this prohibition "on the principle of reciprocity." The first article of the law relating to foreigners' right of ownership of land provides that "a foreigner resident or having domicile in Japan or a foreign juridical person registered in Japan is entitled to have ownership of land, if the law of his own country allows the ownership of land to Japanese subjects or Japanese juridical persons, *provided that the foreign juridical person must obtain the permission of the Minister for Home Affairs before acquiring the ownership of land.*"

Certain exceptions are made as to the lands in certain provinces on the ground that the same are necessary for national defence. This is by no means an exhaustive list of the protection which the Japanese Government extends to the industries and trade of the country.

There are subsidised organisations whose business is to give facilities to Japanese to go to other countries and settle there. The fact is that there is hardly any branch of industrial or commercial activity in Japan in which some kind of initiative has not been taken by the Government, or which was not subsidised by the Government at some stage of its evolution. That explains the wonderful progress made by Japanese industries in such a short time. Even at the present moment it is under consideration to start the manufacture of aniline dyes either as a wholly Government industry or as a subsidised one.

THE JAPANESE PRESS

The newspaper is as old as civilization itself as well as the institution of organized government, but modern journalism is an institution of recent origin, dating from the invention of the printing press in the West, as printing was known to the Asiatics (Chinese) several thousand years ago. The development of the Japanese Press that has taken place within the last 50 years is as wonderful as the development of other modern institutions in Japan during the same period. The first periodical publication which went under the name of a newspaper was printed in Yedo towards the close of the 50th year of the last century. Its contents were mostly translations from Dutch papers, published in Batavia. Three other weekly papers came into existence before the first Japanese daily newspaper made its appearance at Yokohama in 1871. It was called the Yokohama *Mainichi Shimbun*. *Shimbun* in Japanese means a newspaper. It was followed in quick succession by the *Nichi Nichi* in 1872, *Hochi* in 1873, *Yomiuri* in

1874 and others later on. These papers still exist and are published in Tokio, the capital of the Japanese Empire. In the capital alone are published 21 leading dailies, some of which enjoy a circulation of over a quarter of a million. Several daily papers are also published at Osaka, the Manchester of Japan. In 1915 the total number of newspapers published in Japan amounted to 861, and the total number of periodicals including newspapers and magazines, was 2,719.

The Japanese Press is not quite free in theory, as there are legal restrictions imposed on them which, in a way, hamper its freedom. For example: the Japanese Press Law requires every periodical discussing current politics to deposit a security, ranging from 175 to 2,000 yen,* according to the place or, in the case of a periodical, to the frequency of publication. The Government possesses the right of using the deposit in the payment of a fine or in the discharge of other pecuniary obligation that may be imposed on the paper by the decision of a court of law, but the security cannot be touched nor an editor or publisher

* The Yen is equivalent to Re. 1-9-0.

fined except by the decision of the court of law. In that respect the Japanese Press Law is more liberal than the Indian. Moreover the fixing of the security is determined, not by the arbitrary will of the Magistrate, but by definite rules. There is another article of the Japanese Press Law which is rather unique, *viz.*, the procedure which is adopted in the case of private libel. It entitles the party concerned, to oblige the newspaper which published a libel, to insert a contradiction in one of the three following issues, using the same type as that in which the original paragraph appeared and in columns equally conspicuous as those in which the offensive matter was printed. The contradiction must be accompanied by the name and address of the sender and must not exceed the length of the original statement, any excess to be paid for at the journal's usual advertising rates. Failure to comply with these requirements involves the penalty of from yen fifty to one thousand. When a newspaper violates the provision of the Press Law, relating to military or diplomatic censorship in time of emergency, it is liable to suppression by the decision of a court of law. There is no provision in the Japanese Press Law for forfeiture of publications.

Publications can be prohibited or their sale forbidden. Newspapers may be suppressed or suspended under the law by a decision of a court of justice. In 1914, 453 issues of newspapers or publications were suppressed, one was suspended, and there were 114 cases at law courts. Out of those suppressed or of those the sale of which was forbidden in 1914, 135 cases related to diplomatic or military affairs occasioned by the European War. Besides the newspapers and periodicals published in the Japanese language, there are about half a dozen daily papers printed and published in the English language. Most of them are owned and edited by foreigners, but the majority by Englishmen. Their circulation is necessarily limited. Very few Japanese take them. Their circulation is chiefly confined to foreigners residing or travelling in Japan.

From the above it would appear that the Japanese Press is very much hampered by the restrictions imposed by the Press Law, but a few days' residence in Japan, and even a slight acquaintance with the contents of the Japanese papers, makes it clear that in practice the Japanese Press is as free as the press in the Western countries and that, except in the matter of security, the provisions of the Press Law as to prohibition or suppression or suspension are put into operation in only extreme cases. Sometimes the Japanese papers become even more rabid than the Yellow Press in America.

Another feature of the Japanese Press is that there is no prohibition against Government servants owning or writing for the papers. Almost all leading politicians, whether members of Government or in the opposition, have their own organs, owning them wholly or in part.

The opposition papers are as outspoken in their criticism of Government policy and Government measures as the newspapers of the most advanced countries of the West. The members of Government often entertain journalists at dinners or other parties to explain to them the policy of the Government and consult them over national affairs. Members of the opposition Press are as freely invited to these entertainments as of the newspapers of the party in power, or those belonging to neither party. Thus the Press is in close touch with the Government and is taken into confidence on almost every occasion of national emergency. One notices that, more often than not, ministers inviting the press to entertainments fail to impress the opposition Press favourably. Several Japanese papers have their own telegraphic services in the important countries of the world. They subscribe for Reuter's telegrams, too, but generally they depend on their own correspondents in the capitals of the different countries of the world.

The Japanese editor is generally well-informed and up-to-date in world politics. About Indian affairs, they are hopelessly ignorant. The fact is that they do not attach any importance to Indian politics, though of late a departure in this respect has been noticed. The Japanese dailies employ very large staffs. Some of the leading papers have as many as 200 or 300 writers on their staff, from the chief editor downwards. Every daily paper has a foreign department which is staffed by persons who have received their training in and have been to the foreign countries. Similarly there are commerce, literary, and art departments, each in charge of a special staff. The Japanese newspaper man is not, as a rule, paid as well as men holding similar positions in European and American countries. In Tokio, the chief editor of a leading newspaper does not get more than 300 yen a month. I was informed that there is only one newspaper editor in the whole country who gets a salary of 500 yen a month, but this is of course due to the comparatively low standards of wages and living that prevail in the country. And if one considers the number of writers engaged in preparing a newspaper for the press, it appears that the salary is not small and the Japanese newspaper man is as open to other sources of income as the pressman of other Western countries. Almost all important papers depute members of their own staff to the different countries of the world to study their affairs on the spot, thus keeping themselves in close touch with events which happen in other countries and with the under-currents of public opinion which can only be studied by personal and close attention on the spot. There is hardly any important paper in Japan some members of whose staff have not been to foreign countries, all specially deputed by their own paper and at its expense. In fact, every paper keeps one or more of its representatives in the important countries of the world. Compared with the Japanese Press the Indian Press seems to be in a state of infancy yet. Even the best Indian dailies have no representatives in the outside world except London. Very few have London correspondents, most of whom are non-Indians. The London letters of the Indian Press are generally insipid, containing matters which become stale by the time those letters are published. Most of the letters do not contain anything which is not to be found in the Congress Publication "India." In England there are competent Indians who can serve as correspondents of the Indian papers, but the latter seem to have a certain prejudice against them. The fact is that the Indian papers cannot afford to pay for correspondents or contributions from abroad. A genuine, intimate and close study of current politics in foreign countries involves a certain amount of expenditure which is beyond the means of those who ordinarily write for the Indian press from outside. This results in that deplorable ignorance which characterises the Indian papers about the true trend of foreign affairs and their bearing on Indian politics.

The truth of the matter is that the press in India cannot be developed without a much greater development of Indian industries. The press and the trade are inseparable under modern conditions. It is business which maintains the press and not the reading public. Big manufactures, developed industries, high class business alone can advertise on terms which make it possible for the newspapers to sell cheap and extend their circulation and influence. That is what accounts for the development of the Japanese Press. The Indian paper has no such support. It depends chiefly upon its sales and is sold at comparatively high prices, which naturally limits its circulation.

The limited circulation of the Indian newspaper is also due to the general illiteracy which prevails in India. In Japan, almost every man and woman can read and write. In India only 5 p. c. of the population, if you take the figures together, can do so. So the circle of readers is necessarily small. Besides, the Indians have a vicious habit of reading books or papers purchased by others, even though they have the means to make their own purchases. The Indians have yet to learn that a writer is as much entitled to be compensated for his labor as any other class of workers; that literature cannot be developed in a country where people look upon literary efforts as more or less amateur, not entitling the men engaged in this work to be compensated in money. The literary profession is as honorable, if not more, as any other, and unless the men engaged in that profession are supported by the public so as to make them independent of other means of earning their living, the country cannot expect a high class development of its literature. The reading public in India seems to be under the impression that a literary man creates everything from his imagination which they think does not cost him anything. They seem to ignore that a literary man has to invest, as much money, if not more, "in his tools and instruments" as any other kind of industrial worker has to do. The tools of a literary man are ordinarily books and publications from which he gathers his information and which he has to study and digest if he has to make any valuable contribution to his subject.

All this is true of our countrymen. Yet the chief factor in keeping down the circulation of the Indian newspaper is the lack of manufactures and industries, which will pay for advertisements and thus support the press and enable it to sell cheaply. One sometimes wonders how a huge paper, like the *London Times,* can be sold for a penny (equivalent to one anna) and a paper like the *London Daily News* for half a penny (two pice). The American papers are still cheaper. The Sunday Edition of the *New York*

Times or the *San Francisco Examiner* or the Chicago *Tribune* is a heavy load, and it can be had all for five cents (two and half annas in Indian money). Considering the purchasing value of Indian money, the cheapness of the English and the American newspapers is still more remarkable. It is a fact well-known that all these papers would go to bankruptcy if they had to depend for their income on their sales. In fact, some of the papers actually suffer losses by larger sales. Their income is derived from advertisements. Similar is the case in Japan. There the daily papers are perhaps even cheaper than in England and the United States. There are evils, no doubt, connected with this system, but at present we are not considering the ethical side of the question. The growth of the Indian newspaper is decidedly retarded by the backwardness of the country in industries and manufacture. It amuses one and sometimes excites one's laughter as well as pity, to scan the advertisements that appear in the Indian vernacular Press. One is sometimes tempted to think that the only thing on which the Indian vernacular papers thrive, are the specifics for certain unmentionable diseases. We have no doubt that the country is powerless but whether the medicines advertised in the vernacular Press are the proper remedy is doubtful. These advertisements are obscene in the extreme and very objectionable from a moral point of view. Yet even the papers, whose mission is to inculcate purity and morality and spirituality, have to accept these advertisements and make them a prominent feature of their columns. That only shows the poverty of our resources. However, this was only by the by.

I am inclined to think that the proprietors of the Indian newspapers are lacking, to a certain extent at least, in a spirit of enterprise. Some of them are known to have made fortunes in this business. Yet they grudge to invest money in improvements and in getting high class contributions from experts. The Indian paper would do well to club themselves into groups for the purpose of deputing special correspondents to foreign countries and for the purpose of sending the members of their own staff in rotation to study on the spot in the different countries of the world, how the latter have solved the problems which are at the present moment agitating the Indian mind; how India can make money by increasing its trade and how the Indian producer can save the money which at present goes to the pockets of the foreign middle-man. The great problem that faces India is what to do with her young men, and I am certain that if the foreign middle-man could be replaced by Indians, a great field will be opened for the employment of Indians who are at present rotting in Government offices or eking out a miserable living in the crowded profession of law.

A close study of the Japanese Press on the spot leads me to think that the Japanese Press is a great power, perhaps greater than the American Press in America and the English Press in England. The Japanese Ministers make every effort to placate the Press and feel very uncomfortable when they are persistently attacked by the Press. A Press conducted by a few men only is not sufficiently potent to mould and guide public opinion. Its power must eventually depend upon the number and ability of the people who write for it and upon its circulation. Where the newspaper is prepared by a larger number of men than a staff of two or three permanent editors, the public does not feel so much confidence in the opinions expressed by it, as they would if they were conscious that the paper represents the labor of a large number of their countrymen who have devoted time and thought to the writings that make up the paper. This requirement the Japanese Press fulfills; and hence its power over the public and the Government and its vigour.

THE COST OF ADMINISTRATION IN INDIA, JAPAN AND THE UNITED STATES OF AMERICA

It is admitted by all competent observers that India is one of the poorest countries in the world; the average income of an Indian being only 2 pounds a year (10 dollars of American money and 20 yen of Japanese) according to the official estimate made in Lord Curzon's time. A comparison of the salaries paid to the Indian administrators with those paid to men in similar positions in Great Britain, the United States of America and Japan will show that the Indian administration is the most costly in the world.

Before we quote the actual figures we would like to point out that although the exchange value of the Indian Rupee is equal to 33 cents of American money and about 66 sens of the Japanese money (*i.e.*, the American dollar is equal to Rs. 3 and the Japanese Yen equal to Rs. 1½), the economic value of the rupee, judged from the prices of necessaries of life and from the wages of labour, is about equal to that of the

American dollar and the Japanese yen. It is a fact which I know from my personal experience. The purchasing value of the Rupee has gone down much of late, but still it is as good as that of a dollar in America and a yen in Japan.

Central Government.

The President of the United States of America, who ranks with the great royalties of the world in position, gets a salary of 75,000 dollars without any other allowance. The Prime Minister of Japan gets 12,000 yen. The Viceroy and Governor-General of India gets Rs. 2,50,800, besides a very large amount in the shape of allowances. The Cabinet Ministers of the United States get a salary of 12,000 dollars each, that of Japan, 8,000 yen, and the Members of the Viceroy's Council 80,000 Rs. each.

In the whole Federal Government of the United States there are only 3 offices which carry a salary of more than 8,000 dollars a year. They are given below :—

The President of the General Navy Board	...	13,500
Solicitor General	...	10,000
Assistant Solicitor General	...	9,000

All the other salaries range from 2,100 to 8,000 dollars. In the State Department all offices, including those of the secretaries, carry salaries of 2,100 to 5,000 dollars. In the Treasury Department the Treasurer gets 8,000, and 3 other officers get 6,000 each. All the remaining get from 2,500 to 5,000 dollars. In the War Department there are only two offices which have a salary of 8,000 each attached to them, *viz.*, that of Chief of Staff and of Quarter Master General. The rest get from 2,000 to 6,000. In the Navy Department, besides the president of the General Board mentioned above, the President of the Naval Examination Board gets 8,000 and so does the Commandant of the Marine Corps. All the rest get from 6,000 downwards. In the Department of Agriculture there is only one office carrying a salary of 6,000. All the rest, from 5,000 downwards. The Chief of the Weather Bureau (an expert) gets 6,000. In the Commerce Department 4 experts get 6,000 each, the rest from 5,000 downwards. These are annual salaries.

In Japan the officials of the Imperial Household have salaries ranging from 5,500 to 8,000 yen, officials of the Higher Civil Service from 3,700 to

4,200 a year, Vice-Ministers of State 5,000, chief of the Legislative Bureau 5,000, the Chief Secretary of the Cabinet 5,000, the Inspector-General of Metropolitan Police 5,000.

President of the Board of Audit ...	6,000
President of the Administrative Litigation Court	6,000
President of the Railway Board ...	7,500
President of the Privy Council ...	6,000
Vice-President of the Privy Council ...	5,500

and so on. All the salaries are per annum.

India.

President of the Railway Board gets ...	60,000 or 72,000 Rs.
Two Members of the Railway Board ...	48,000 each
Secretaries in the Army, Public Works and Legislative Departments	42,000 each
Secretaries in Finance, Foreign, Home, Revenue and Agriculture	

and Commerce and Industry Departments	48,000
Secretary in the Education Department ...	36,000
(The Chief Commissioner of Education in the United States gets only	5,000 Dollars.)
Joint Secretary ...	30,000
Controller and Auditor General ...	42,000
Accountants General from	27,000 to 33,000
Commissioner of Salt Revenue ...	30,000
Director-General of Post and Telegraph from	36,000 to 42,000

(In the United States the Post Master General is a Cabinet Minister and gets 12,000 dollars). Post Masters General from 18,000 to 24,000.

Among the officers directly under the Government of India there are only a few who get salaries below Rs. 20,000, most of the others get from Rs. 20,400 to 36,000. The fact that the population of the United States of America consists of people of all races from the world and that there is a constant flow of immigration makes the work of administration very difficult and complex; otherwise also the administrative problems handled by the United States administration are even more complex and difficult than those faced by the administration in India.

Provincial Administrations.

The United States Government have under it 54 States, some of which are as big in area as, if not bigger than the several provinces of India. The Governors of these States are paid from 2,500 dollars a year up to 12,000 dollars a year. There is only one State, that of Illinois, which pays 12,000 to its Governor, five others, amongst them California and New York, pay 10,000; only two, Massachusettes and Indiana, pay 8,000 and only one pays 7,000; 3 pay 6,000; the rest all 5,000 or less. There is only one territory under the United States Government, viz., that of the Phillipines, which pays a salary of 20,000 to its Governor-General. In India the Governors of Madras, Bombay and Bengal, each receive 1,20,000 rupees per year, besides large amounts for allowances. Lieutenant-Governors receive Rs. 1,00,000 each, besides allowances. The Chief Commissioner receives 62,000 in Assam, 62,000 in Central Provinces and Berar, 36,000 in Delhi, and so on. The Political Residents in the Native States receive from 33,000 to 48,000, besides allowances. In Japan the Governors of Provinces are paid at the rate of from 3,700 to 4,500 yens per year, besides allowances varying from 400 to 600 yen per year. The provincial services in India are paid on a similarly lavish scale. In Bengal the salaries range from 4,800 rupees a year allowed to an Assistant Magistrate and Collector to Rs. 64,000 allowed to members of council, and the same may be said of the other provinces also. Coming to the judiciary we find that the Judges of the Supreme Court of the United States get a salary of 14,500 dollars each, the Chief Justice getting 15,000; the circuit judges get a salary of 7,000 dollars each, the District Judges $ 6,000 each. In the State of New York, the Judges of the Supreme Court belonging to the General Sessions get 17,500 each and those of the Speci.l Sessions get from 9,000 to 10,000 each, City Magistrates get a salary of 7,000 to 8,000 each. In India the Chief Justice of Bengal gets 72,000, the Chief Justices of Bombay, Madras and the United

Provinces get 60,000 each. The Chief Judges of the Chief Courts of the Punjab and Burmah get 48,000 each and the Puisne Judges of the High Courts the same amount, the Puisne Judges of the Chief Courts getting 42,000. In the Province of Bengal the salaries of the District and Sessions Judges range from 24,000 to 36,000 a year. The salaries of the District Judges in the other major provinces range from 20,000 to 36,000 and so on. The Deputy Commissioners in India get a salary according to different scales in different provinces varying from 18,000 to 27,000 a year ; the Commissioners getting from 30,000 to 36,000 a year. In Japan the Appeal Court Judges and Procurators get salaries varying from 1,200 to 5,000 yen per year. Only one officer, that of the President of the Court of Cassation, getting 6,000. The District Court Judges and Procurators are paid at the rate of 750 to 3,700 yen per year.

It is needless to compare the salaries of the minor offices in the three countries. The fact that the Indian taxpayer has to pay so heavily for the European Services engaged in the work of administration makes it necessary that even the Indian officers should be paid on a comparatively high scale, thus raising the cost of administration to the highest pitch and telling very injuriously on the condition of the men in the lowest grades of the Government service. The difference between the salaries of the officers and the men forming the rank and file of the Government offices in the three countries mentioned above shows how the ordinary Government servant in the lowest rank in India suffers from the fact that the officers have to be paid at such high rates. We will illustrate what we mean.

The Police.

Police Force of New York City.—The Chief Inspector gets $3,500 a year, Captains $2,750 each, Lieutenants $2,250, Sergeants 1,750. Patrol men, corresponding to our Constables, 1,400 each. The Commissioner of Police gets $7,500. In Japan the Inspector-General of the Metropolitan Police gets 5,000 yen. The figures for the lower offices are not available, but the minimum salary of a constable is 13 yen per month, besides which he gets his equipment, uniform and boots, etc., free. In India the Inspectors General get from 24,000 to 36,000, Deputy Inspectors General from 18,000 to 21,600, District Superintendents of Police from 8,000 to 14,400,

Assistants from 3,600 to 6,000, Inspectors from 1,800 to 3,000, Sub-Inspectors from 600 to 1,200, Head Constables from 180 to 240, *Constables from* Rs. 120 to 144 per year. We have taken these figures from the Indian Year Book published by the Times of India Office, Bombay. We know as a fact that the Police Constables in the Punjab are paid from 8 to 10 rupees a month, that is, from 96 to 120 rupees a year. The reader would mark the difference between grades of salaries from the highest to the lowest in India as compared with the United States and Japan. While in India the lowest grade servants are frightfully underpaid, the highest grade officers are paid on a lavish scale. In the other countries of the world this is not the case.

Educational Department.—In the United States (we quote the figures of the New York City) the lowest school teachers get a salary of 720 dollars a year rising to 1,500. In the upper grades the maximum salaries are 1,820 to 2,260. Principals of Elementary Schools receive 3,500 and Assistants 2,500. In High Schools salaries range from 900 to 3,150 dollars. In Training Schools from 1,000 to 3,250 dollars. Principals of High Schools and Training Schools are paid 5,000 dollars and the same salary is paid to the District Superintendents. The salary of the Commissioner of Education in New York is 7,500 dollars. In Japan the Minister of Education, who is a Cabinet Minister, gets a salary of 8,000 yen per year and the lowest salary of a teacher ranges from 16 yen to 18 yen per month. In the United States the highest salaries allowed to College Professors are from 5,000 to 7,000 dollars a year. In Japan they range from 600 to about 4,000 yen per year. Coming to India we find that while the administrative officers and even the Professors get fairly high salaries, the teachers in the schools are miserably underpaid. We do not believe there is a single country in the world where the difference between the remunerations allowed to the highest and the lowest of the state servants is so disproportionate as in India, yet there is a tendency to still further increase the salaries of the high officials, European and Indian, while even very insignificant increases to the salaries of the lowest servants of the State are very grudgingly allowed. Then the high officials get so many kinds of allowances that sometimes the amount of those allowances equals their salaries, which is not the case in the case of the lower grade servants. The fact is that the Government in India does not attach sufficient importance to the ordinary man. His needs are often overlooked in the desire to please the higher services and to keep them contented. Considering that every man in India is supposed to have a family, the condition of the lowest official is extremely miserable and justifies corruption in their ranks. The Government of India must know it, yet they have not done anything to remedy this state of things. A rise in the prices is claimed to be a good ground for raising the salaries of the highly paid civilians, but the same weight is not attached to it when the question of a rise in the salaries in the lower grades arises. In the latter case the unfeeling argument of the market rate is freely applied, and it is argued that it will be unbusinesslike for Government to pay more for services which can be secured cheaper.

The figures relating to military services in India are not available but we know that the above remarks have as much force in the case of military services as in that of the civil.

OUR EDUCATION

THE more an *educated* Indian mixes with foreigners in Europe and America, the more keenly does he feel the defects of his education. The consciousness of comparative ignorance and lack of proper upbringing creeps on him bit by bit, and gets on his nerves. He begins to look down upon himself and therein faces a great danger which in this age of *boastful self-confidence* (grown almost to a science in the West), is real and substantial. This age has no use for meekness and humility or for self-sacrifice in the oriental sense. This is an age of self-assertion. We are living in times when "*boosting*," self-laudation, and self-advertising pays. It will not do for us to make too much of our shortcomings and defects. That breeds want of confidence and leads to dependence. Fully conscious of that, I cannot help taking my countrymen into my confidence, as to how I feel about the so-called education we receive in our schools and colleges.

In this respect, private institutions maintained and managed by non-official agencies are as bad as, if not worse than, Government institutions. Oftener than not, the former are only a bad copy of the latter. Competing for the honors of University examinations and Governmental recognition, they neglect the special objects for which they were started, or the special mission which they have in the education of the nation. Everything in India must bear the stamp of Government approval or the seal of Government recognition, and the managers of the private schools have neither the time nor the inclination nor even the means to disregard it. Having been closely connected with the management of the Dayanand Anglo-Vedic College at Lahore, from its very conception up to 1910, covering the best part of my life and a period of over a quarter of a century, I know how the managers are forced by circumstances to drift downstream. They start with grand ideas, about absolute self-help, and independence of official control and official approval. Visions of national education, physical education and many other kinds of education, are requisitioned for the collection of funds and an appeal to the public. Bit by bit, however, it begins to dawn on them, that they had counted without their host; that to create a demand for the sort of education they want to impart, they will have to toil and wait for years before they can show any results. The collection of funds, however, depends on results. So in seeking for immediate results they start by *postponing* action on their principles, pending the accumulation of funds, until at last the funds and the popularity of the institution become their sole or at least principal objects. The needs of the nation and the principles of sound education, for which they had started, fall into the background.

In the meantime, the demands of the Department of Public Instruction and then the demands of the University begin to tell heavily, and gradually their approval becomes one of the mainsprings, if not the only mainspring, of their conduct. At first the Department and the University try underhand means to kill their independence, but eventually they stait on a campaign of reconciliation by a combination of recognition and threats. This last proves effectual, so effectual, that it brings the managers to their knees, making them almost abject in their submission. Then the last chain in the link is put on, *viz.*, an appeal to the personal ambitions of the conductors, which brings an utter collapse of the principles which had inspired the founders. Let me not be misunderstood. I have the highest respect for the managers of the D. A.-V. College. One of them I idolize; the others I love. It is not my object to criticise or to find fault with them. What I maintain is that the circumstances are such as to make it almost impossible to resist. As one of those who guided or controlled the destinies of the College for a quarter of a century, I assume the fullest responsibility for the drift downwards. There are other institutions in the country which started with similar principles but which have failed to keep up to their spirit. The struggle is unequal and I do not blame them for their failure. The most recent of them is the Hindu University experiment. With the constitution of its governing body and with the history of its foundation before us, it would be unreasonable to build any big hopes on it. The Hindu University will have fine buildings, may have a fine staff, but it can only be a Hindu edition of the other Universities in India. The incidents connected with its opening ceremony are not very inspiring. It is almost impossible to bring about a radical change in the system of education in India, unless there is a substantial change in the attitude of the Government towards education and in their educational policy. The remedy is in the hands of Government and Government alone. The education of a nation cannot be undertaken, even to a moderate degree, by private agencies, however enterprising and spirited the latter may be.

But what are the principal defects which make us feel so small in the presence of the foreign educated person?

Firstly, our education has no marketable value outside India. Even in India it makes us absolutely dependent on Government, or on professions which are after all so much allied with the work of administration, *viz.*, law, teaching, or office-work, as to justify their being styled semi-Governmental. The full significance or insignificance of this kind of education is not felt and properly realized unless one faces the necessity of earning a livelihood anywhere outside of India. I have seen practical illustrations of it in the U. S. A. An Indian matriculate, or F. A. passed, or Bachelor of Arts finds that the only way by which he can earn a livelihood in the U. S. A., if the expected remittance from home does not arrive, or is delayed or even stopped, is by seeking a job to wash dishes, attend on the table, do menial work in families or go out in the fields or on the roads as an unskilled laborer. Even here he finds that he is greatly handicapped by the education he had received in his native country. He was never trained to work with his hands. After 10 or 15 years of literary education received in Indian schools or colleges he finds it extremely hard to learn the use of his hands for the purpose of washing dishes or sweeping the room or doing other kinds of daily work in open fields or on roads. That so many of them are eventually able to earn *something* to keep themselves going, is very creditable to their power of endurance. But it is pathetic to see men of education being bossed by absolutely illiterate countrymen of theirs who fare much better in manual labour. Their practical knowledge of agriculture does them good service. Then their physical condition is always better than that of the so-called educated men. So the former are heads of gangs and the latter work under them and put up with all sorts of humiliation.

An educated Hindu is generally at sea if he has to earn his living anywhere outside of the province of his birth. He is besides helpless like a baby in several other respects. Very rarely, if at all, does he know anything of cooking, of stitching, or of first-aid. Most of them can neither swim nor row. They do not know even the rudiments of the art of self-defence, because no one has ever devoted a thought to that part of their education. The only thing they know is the use of the English language for ordinary purpose. This, no doubt, saves them from being altogether stranded in countries where English is spoken.

Secondly, looking at the cultural side of education, they have no notion of it. They have no ear for music; nor any eye for a picture or a painting. The Bengalees and the Mahrattas, thanks to their family influences, are better in this respect than the Punjabees or the U. P. men. Ask a Northern Indian to entertain an audience and it is a sight to see him making excuses. He cannot sing; he cannot play; he cannot recite; he cannot even tell a story. Take him to a concert or an exhibition of Fine Arts and he feels as if he is in a prison. He cannot appreciate, nor enjoy, nor admire. In his lonely hours he does not know how to relieve the monotony of his solitude by humming a tune. The only thing he can do is to prattle of the past greatness of India without even knowing what that greatness consisted in, or sometimes to sneer at it. A Punjabee youth is a pathetic sight in a group of boys and girls determined on "*good time.*" He can make no contribution to the common mirth of the party. He can only sigh. Asked to recite some poetry, he may be able to repeat a few verses of Tennyson or Shakespeare in humble accents. But as to Punjabee poetry or Urdu poetry or Sanskrit or Hindi poetry, he never considered himself so foolish as to waste time on it. The folklore of his country, he has never heard of. Sometimes he meets foreign gentlemen or ladies who know of his country's folklore or mythology better than himself, and then his humiliation or discomfiture knows no bounds.

We hear all kinds of theories put forward by the rulers of India to improve the quality of the education imparted in Indian schools and colleges, but when we come to practical measures we find them exhausted in exaggerated emphasis on good buildings, a slight increase in the salaries of teachers and great emphasis on a superior and a better knowledge of English. The Indian administrators' standard of excellence of education is generally measured by the scholars' proficiency in English language and literature. In their eyes that alone is the principal aim of an Indian's education. We often hear of Sir James Meston's thundering on quality in preference to quantity, but we have not been told what *is* his standard of quality. We do not know if the U. P. Schools are now, since Sir James Meston's accession to the Office of the Lieutenant-Governor of the United Provinces of Oudh and Agra, turning out better men, than before—men better able to fight the battle of life vocationally, men who will be able to earn a living in any country and under any circumstances, men with a knowledge of the foreign languages of the world, men with finer tastes and finer bodies. When one compares the educational methods in India with those prevailing in Japan, one is inclined to think that we in India are 50 years behind Japan, though the Japanese in their turn are no less than 25 years behind Europe and America. The Japanese education makes an ample provision both for mind and body. Their system of physical culture is perfect. They insist on a young man learning the art of self-defence to perfection. They teach him fencing, boxing, archery, shooting, swimming and running. All kinds of schools, religious or secular, general or professional, common or special, vie with one another in the provision they make for physical culture. They amply provide for Tennis, Cricket, Football, Hockey and Baseball, but what they insist on, are the games that make a man efficient for offence as well as defence. Then, every Japanese lad knows how to sing and play and how to draw. They have an instinct for beauty, but the development of the taste to perfection is done by education. It is a part of a young Japanese's education to know something of everything for the ordinary needs of life—a bit of cooking, a bit of sewing and stitching, and so on. The Japanese are at the present moment everywhere on earth, from the North Pole to the South Pole, from Japan to California. They are readily accepted in domestic service and so are the Chinese; but the Hindus (including the Mohammedans) are so clumsy that it is with difficulty they find a job to keep their souls and bodies together. Why? Because they are lacking in the training which makes a man useful, even though he may not be an expert in any particular line.

I am sure we want Sanskrit scholars and scholars of the English language. We want scientists, philosophers, doctors, jurists, historians, economists, scholars in every branch of human knowledge, but above all, what we want are sensible men who can look to their ordinary needs and comforts under any circumstances in which they may be placed; men who can depend on themselves when cornered; men who can turn a pie by laying their hands to anything which may come handy in time of need. That is the kind of education upon which the edifice of higher and a university education should be raised. Even in the higher spheres what the country needs more than anything else are better mechanics, more efficient carpenters, skilful electricians, resourceful chemists, men who will enable the country to compete with the outside world in the output of their industries. The promoters and leaders of the Hindu University cannot put the country's money in their hands to a better use than lead in laying the foundation of a useful system of education. We have quite enough of grammarians or lexicographers or orators,—men who can talk a lot about philosophy and religion and spirituality but who fail to realize that a hungry stomach is not the best condition for sound thought. A nation, helpless, dependent, wanting in common sense, looking to others for the necessities of life, can only *talk* of religion but they can never *live* it. We have had enough and to spare of *the philosophy of religion.*

What we now need is a *living* religion which will inspire us to nobler deeds and higher ideals in the life of the world in which we live and breathe, than in the life which is known to occultists and clairvoyants only. We want thought but even more life. We want spirit, but just now, even more body. We want high ideals, but even more, practical ideals. For God's sake, let us not put the cart before the horse.

The world has enough of admiration for our philosophy, for our mysticism, for the knowledge of the spirit developed by our ancestors. Yet they hold us in contempt all the same, as we are lacking in those things which go for self-respect, self-assertion, self-confidence and self-dependence. It is a critical time in the life of our nation, and we cannot be too careful in laying out ideals for *immediate realization* and in chalking out lines of national activities for the amelioration of the condition of our people. In our present condition we are the most despised people on the face of the earth. Even our educated men fail to inspire respect because of the lack of true education.

Oh! Our Education! Is it not tragic that we should at times feel that in the battle of life we might have done better without it.

IS NOT THE EAST A UNITY AS COMPARED WITH THE WEST?

SOME superficial observers think that the East is not a unity, as implied in the familiar antithesis of East and West; that while the East is not a unity, the modern West is, and that between India on the one hand, and China or Japan, on the other, there is as great a difference as between India and any western country. Those who know the East well, have lived in India, China and Japan for a number of years and have studied the religious and social life of the people carefully, know that the statement is not an accurate description of things as they are. But to an oriental himself, be he a Hindu, a Chinese or a Japanese, whose knowledge of the East is not confined to his own country and who has travelled in other countries with eyes open, the statement is ludicrous. Why, there is more unity of thought and life in the East to-day than there has ever been in the West at any time.

Now, let us first clear up what we mean by the expressions the East and the West. The writer (Mr. Lowes Dickinson of Cambridge, England), whose views have been quoted in the opening sentence of this paper is thinking of Europe and America as the *West* and India, China and Japan as the *East*. We do not know if he includes the countries of Western Asia also in his conception of the West or if he just ignores them. From the description of the West that he gives in his paper, one is inclined to think that he does not include Western Asia in his conception of the West and simply ignores them. For the purpose of this paper I shall follow his example, though I am prepared to go further and argue that fundamentally there is as much unity in the life of Asia, excluding Russia, as there is in the life of the West as represented by Europe.

The next thing to be cleared up, is, what is meant by "Unity" : The writer in question says :

> "Throughout Europe and America there is the same civilisation, intellectual and economic, so that to a philosophic observer, national boundaries there already begin to appear obsolete and irrelevant."

So,* that is his idea of the unity of the West,.

*This was of course written before the war.

though he is careful to add that this *Modern West* is a very recent creation, in fact, of the last century only. "If one goes back in history," he adds, "we can find more analogy between East and West than now appears."

"Feudal Europe, for example, was in many respects similar to feudal Japan; and a medieval Christian Mystic hardly distinguishable from a contemporary Indian Saint. So the contrast between the Modern West and the West of the Middle Ages is perhaps as great as the contrast between Modern West and India."

Put in sequence, then, the idea resolves itself into the following propositions :

(1) The unity of the Modern West is a creation of the last century only.

(2) The basis of that unity is '*the same civilisation, intellectual and economic.*'

(3) Before the last century, there was more analogy between the East and the West than now, which means that the last century has destroyed or reduced that analogy.

(4) That, now, while there is such a thing as the "West," there is no such thing as the "East." Between India, on the one hand, and China or Japan,

on the other, there is as great a difference as between India and any western country.

We have no quarrel with the first three propositions of the writer, but we demur to the accuracy of the 4th. If the writer means that the last century has wrought so many changes in the East as to dissolve its unity altogether, we do not agree with him. If he means that that unity is being undermined and is in the process of dissolution we might accede to the possibility of it, though with doubts and significant qualifications. It is not, however, clear what he means, because at the outset he says :

> "I shall endeavour to characterise each of the civilisations, first, as they were before her contact with the West and afterwards to consider the effect upon them of the contact."

So he sets out to compare the *West* with India as she was before her contact with the West, as well as with her as modified by that contact.

As regards India Mr. Dickinson is positive that she has a distinct individuality of her own which creates a profound gulf between her and the West. This is an admission of Indian unity which Indians will appreciate regardless of the grounds on which it is based. If I had to prove merely that the writer was wrong in his conclusions about the fundamental differences of India, China and Japan, I would simply show that the circumstances which in his opinion created such a gulf between India and the West, were shared in by China and Japan, as well. I, however, propose to do more than this. I want to establish that even at the present moment there is a fundamental unity between India, China and Japan, and that the western influences over these countries have not yet advanced sufficiently far to destroy that unity; that the said influences are, everywhere, in these countries, producing more or less the same results and threatening to make the East a bad and imperfect copy of the West, and that in order to maintain their individual character, as well as their continental character, they shall have to struggle hard against the levelling influences of the West. If the wholesale adoption of the western civilisation in all its phases be the sole test of the peoples' progress then no doubt Japan has had an advantage over the other countries and has seemingly absorbed more of the western civilisation than the other two, but whoever dips deeper into the life of the people of Japan finds sufficient to justify the conclusion that Japan is still fundamentally Eastern or Oriental. Of course, India, China and Japan have, each of them, their own distinguishing traits and characteristics and so have the different countries of Europe and America. In the opinion of the writer quoted above, what makes the West *a Unity*, is the sameness of intellectual and economic civilisation. What makes the East *a Unity*, is the sameness of their religious, intellectual and social outlook, and in a manner also, the sameness of their economic life. In the opinion of Mr. Lowes Dickinson, the dominant note of India is religion, and from the way he writes one may legitimately infer that in his opinion India is the only country in the world, that is *really religious*. Discussing what is religion to the mass of the people he says :

"I think it is clear that to the peasants of most countries of Italy, say, or of China or of Japan, religion is no more than a ritual which they would be uncomfortable if they did not perform ; a kind of lightning conductor for the emotions and desires that are concerned with the ordinary business of life, with getting one's living, with birth, marriage, child-bearing and death."

What, however, strikes him as remarkable is that

to the Indians religion is something more than this. He shares the opinion of other observers that even the Indian peasant does really believe that the true life is a spiritual life; that he respects the saint more than any other man; and that he regards the material world as "unreal" and all its cares as "illusion." Having made the general statement Mr. Lowes Dickinson proceeds to show categorically how the Indian religion is radically different from the religion of the western nations. In the first place, he says:

"India has never put Man in the centre of the universe. In India, and wherever Indian influence has penetrated, it is, on the one hand, the tremendous forces of nature, and what lies behind them, that is the object of worship and of speculation, and, on the other hand, Mind and Spirit, not the mind or spirit of the individual person, but the universal Mind, or Spirit, which is in him, but to which he can only have access by philosophic meditation and ascetic discipline. Indian religion is thus very "inhuman" compared to Christianity and very much more in harmony with the spirit of western science than with that of western religion. Man, in the Indian vision, is a plaything and slave of natural forces; only by becoming superman does he gain freedom and deliverance."

Secondly :

"To an Indian saint or philosopher the whole world of matter is unreal, and the whole of human history illusory. There is no meaning in time or the processes of time, still less is there any goodness in it. In some way, unexplained and inexplicable, the terrible illusion we call life dominates mankind. To be delivered from the illusion, from life, that is, activity in time, is the object of all effort and all religion. In this sense the Indian religion is pessimistic. There is, of course, an important distinction between Buddhism and the Brahminism, it supplanted for a time and then succumbed to. Gautama Buddha, it would seem, was a thorough-going sceptic and rationalist ; he believed neither in God nor in the soul ; and the object of his teaching was to deliver men from life to annihilation by instructing them how to eliminate desire. *Brahminism, on the other hand, wishes to deliver them from false life to true life. The true life is life eternal : and we may have access to it by discipline and meditation.* But from my immediate point of view this distinction is not important. What is important is that, in either form, precisely that is denied which the West most emphatically affirms,—the *reality and importance of the material world, and of the historic process in time.* The West is often called materialistic as compared with the East. But this antithesis, so far as it is true, does not depend on any metaphysical view held or denied as to the nature of matter. *The West does not profess to know what matter is, and its hypotheses about it are always changing.* The real point of distinction is, that the west believes that all effort ought to centre upon the process of living in time ; that the process has reality and significance ; and that the business of religion *is not to deliver us from effort by convincing us of its futility, but to sanctify and justify it.*"

It is very difficult to find any very clear line of distinction between Mr. Dickinson's first point of contrast and that which is his second. Put in simple language it comes to this that the Indian religion denies the realities of this world, calls life and its manifestations illusory and aims at saving men by reducing them to nothing; the western religion on the other hand affirms the reality of the world and insists upon right action in this life. In other words, the Indian religion is "inhuman" while the religion of the West is human. At this stage one feels forced to ask what the religion of the western nations is. Is it Christianity or something different? Mr. Dickinson's answer is equivocal. He says yes as well as no. At first he assumes that it is so, but when he is confronted with the fact that "Christianity too has this idea of the illusoriness of the world," which he considers to be the dominant note of the Indian religion, he at once shifts his position and says that "the western nations have never really been Christians. Their true religion has only become apparent as Christianity has declined." What then is their religion? "That religion," he replies, "not yet expressed in form but implicit in their conduct, is that the time process is also the real process; and that everything material matters very much indeed; and that spiritualism must either recognise the claims of matter or retire from the conflict and that the life and its purposes are significant and important and what a man ought to attend to." "This," Mr. Dickinson adds, "is the real postulate of the Modern West; and that is what all Indian religion and philosophy has denied." In contrasting the "inhumanity" of the Hindu religion with Christianity, Mr. Dickinson had said only a while ago that the Hindu "religion was more in harmony with the spirit of western science than that of western religion."* Are we then to suppose that *"the*

*Compare it with the statement on p. 45, "What is most characteristic and profound in the Indian spirit is antagonistic to and irreconcilable with rationalism and science."

western religion is not in harmony with the spirit of western science?" If so, wherefrom does that religion emanate, if it is neither Christianity nor in harmony with the spirit of modern science? The people of the West are not likely to accept either of Mr. Dickinson's statements. They would probably say that Christianity as interpreted in the terms of modern science is the religion of the West. In which case either it does not materially differ from Hinduism or Mr. Dickinson's statement that Hinduism is more in harmony with the spirit of western science than with western religion is untenable.

The truth is that all attempts to generalise on questions like this are bound to land a man in awkward positions. Mr. Dickinson's conception of the Hindu religion is fundamentally wrong, though it is correct as regards certain phases of it. These phases are the manifestations of that thought-current which gave birth to Buddhism. Buddhist doctrine, as such, has not many followers in India proper to-day, though it is true that popular Hinduism bears on its face many marks of Buddhistic influence. The Vedanta of Shankara may in a way be said to be a Vedic development of Buddhism, made consistent with the idea of a Universal Supreme Soul which Shankara founds on the teachings of the Vedas. Mr. Dickinson admits that the Vedas "*reflect an attitude to life similar to that of the Western Aryans; but this essentially active, positive and optimistic view* gradually clouds over" and is replaced, Mr. Dickinson will have us believe, "by a view which depicts the world of matter as unreal and the whole of human history as illusory." Mr. Dickinson also admits that the view of life propounded by Brahmanism is materially different from Buddhism. Brahmanism, according to Mr. Dickinson, wishes to deliver man from false life to true life. It declares that true life is life eternal and we may have access to it by discipline and meditation. His statement of Brahmanism is essentially incomplete and imperfect but whatever it is it is inconsistent with the idea that life is "illusory" and "unreal."

So the general statements made by Mr. Dickinson are open to serious objections and any conclusions based on such statements can not but be faulty.

Personally I am inclined to think that there is nothing either in the West or in the East which creates a profound gulf between them, tending to keep them apart from each other for ever. What gulf there is, has been created by the modern development of the West within the last two hundred years—a development which has been denied to the East. This gulf is destined to be removed or abridged as soon as circumstances allow the East to assimilate the material civilisation of the West and come into line with it intellectually. In a few decades, if not in a few years, the economic life of the world is likely to become uniform in its fundamentals. That may not be a gain to humanity as such, but such is the march of events that nothing can prevent its realisation and Mr. Dickinson also thinks the same way. As for the intellectual outlook, it is possible that on fuller education and proper appreciation of its distinguishing traits, the East might retain what has always distinguished it from the West. On the other hand it is equally possible that the West might modify its intellectual outlook so as to reduce its angularities to their lowest level and come nearer the Eastern view-points. It would be a good thing for humanity, if the East and the West were to come nearer to each other and understand each other more than they do at present, and thus remove or at any rate reduce the causes of friction and misunderstanding between them, but it will make the world poorer and much less interesting, if it brings about a depressing monotony and a dull ugly uniformity in the life and thought of the East and the West. That the East must imbibe something of the aggressive spirit of the West and must also adopt and assimilate the intellectual achievements of the West if she wants to regain her self-respect, goes without saying, but it would be nothing short of calamity to her as well as to humanity at large if she goes so far as to lose her individuality and become either a copy or a duplicate of the West. Having thus stated, how far in my judgment it is desirable that the East and the West should come near each other, I will now proceed to examine into what constitutes the individuality of India and how far that is shared by China and Japan.

According to Mr. Dickinson there is an important distinction between Buddhism and Brahmanism. That distinction has been pointed out above. According to that distinction the true life is life eternal and we may have access to it by discipline, meditation, knowledge and right conduct, all combined together, and supporting each other. Brahmanism does not deny the reality and importance of the material world. On the other hand it lays stress upon the fact that nobody can be saved except by and through his acceptance of the material world. Says Mr. C. F. Andrews :

"But such exaggerations (he means the exaggerations involved in the view of Indian religion taken by Mr. Dickinson) do not belong to the best that India has produced. They are not the teaching of the Upanishads, or the Bhagavad-Gita. They do not belong to the religious heart of India which has been stirred from age to age by great reforming saints such as Kabir and Tulsi Das. Life, in these writings, is not an empty nothingness, a mere nightmare. Rather, it is pulsing and throbbing with the rhythm of the Universe : it is the vehicle of God's own revelation of himself. *Anandarupam Amritam Yadvibhati:* "God manifests Himself in deathless forms which His joy assumes." Man, in these writings, is not impotent and insignificant. Rather, he is able from the depth of his inner consciousness to say, *Aham asmi,* I AM. History is not meaningless. Rather, it is the utterance of God's voice. The greatest of all Indian books of popular religion are epic histories. The centre of worshipful adoration in North India, among a hundred millions, is Rama, the hero king, the ideal son, husband, father, brother : and Sita, the ideal wife. Last of all, activity, in all the highest forms of Hindu thought, is not banned but cultivated and cherished '—Kurvanneveha karmani jijivishet shatam samah,' says the Isa-upanishad : "Only in the midst of activity wilt thou desire to live a hundred years." The Hindu saints, who are still revered and loved, were not solitary recluses, but men of quickened activities and inspiring deeds."

Mr. Dickinson's statements about the religion of India are not altogether true. But for our present purposes we will assume the correctness of Mr. Dickinson's conclusions and admit for the sake of argument that the dominating note of popular Hindu religion in India to-day is what he says. It is evident then that this dominating note has been supplied by Buddhism or by the influence of Buddhism upon Brahmanism. In that case, is it not true that Buddhism is the key to the intellectual and religious culture of the Far East? Mr. Dickinson could not have studied Japan and China thoroughly to come to the conclusion that the religion of Japan and China was a negligible quantity in the formation of their national character. The evident mistake which Mr. Dickinson has made is this that while he exaggerates the importance and the significance of changes brought about by contact with the West in China and Japan, he unconsciously underestimates the same influence in India. I am not inclined to blame him for that. Japan is a small country which gives the appearance of being compact and homogeneous in the western sense of the term. While India is a huge subcontinent where the influence of the West upon the mass of the people is not noticeable except to a very close observer. In China it is still less. An intimate acquaintance with Japanese life, mixing with the masses in their homes, and attending their religious festivals and religious ceremonies, brings home the wonderful unity of thought and sentiment between India and Japan. To a superficial observer the same note of pessimism, which the Europeans ascribe to Buddhism, is discernable. To a close observer it appears that Shintoism, modified by Buddhism and *vice versa,* has produced the same intellectual and religious atmosphere in Japan as Brahmanism influenced by Buddhism has done in India. But in any case there is more Buddhism and of the Buddhist view of life in China and Japan than in India: while Japan and China have thousands of Buddha temples, India has only a few; while Japan and China have hundreds of thousands of Buddhist priests, monks and teachers, India has not even tens.

In India Buddhist worship and ritual is practically dead. In Japan and China it is a living thing.

Brahmanism in India, Shintoism in Japan and Confucianism in China have a great deal in common. They are united in the importance which they attach to ancestor worship, and ancestor worship still rules the intellectual, the moral and the religious life of the masses of the three nations. An observer who omits to notice that, is not entitled to much credit fo. accurate observation.

The stoical character of practical Taoism is depicted by Chwang in the following words :*

"My pupils, take the attitude of doing nothing, and all beings will of themselves develop (their goodness). Mortify your bodies ; cast out from you the operations of your perceptive senses ; forget your relations with other beings ; cultivate the greatest similarity with the universal ether ; set free your will and deliver your soul (shen) ; be nobody or nothing, and behave as if you had no soul."

"All this is occultism or mysticism ; but it was actually practised, and influenced the ways and life of men. It was far more than theoretical speculation indulged in by a few philosophers ; else we would be

*Religion in China by De Groat, p. 128.

sure to find in Chinese books remains of other systems of thought and behaviour, but there is nothing of the kind. We must perforce assume the existence of one single catholic system, Taoist, embracing the thinking element of ancient China, and a considerable number of men who actually followed its discipline."

The practical note is supplied by ancestor worship. The two combined form the popular religion of the East. The family life, the tribal life, the social life and its amenities are all based on ancestor worship. The extraordinary respect which all East expects its children to show towards their parents, the complicated net of duties which is woven on that idea, obtrudes itself in every phase of life. The joint family system in all its consequences is the natural outcome of it and the jointness of the family is still the normal life in Asia.

The laws dealing with property, with succession, adoption, guardianship, minority and majority, marriage, etc., are all founded on the same notion and there is an astounding similarity in them throughout the East, especially in India, China, Japan, Burma and Siam. Of course there are some differences but the fundamental basis is the same. Modern conditions of life and the introduction of western ideals have effected changes which are likely to have far-reaching effects in the future. But just at the present there does not seem to be much difference between the thought and the practice of the masses in India from that of the masses in Japan and other countries of the East.

Japan has no doubt thrown away her caste system, but that is only an occurence of recent days. This is a difference which is created exclusively by the necessity of political life. The National Government in Japan has materially contributed to this reform; and as Japan was a small country, the reform took effect more rapidly and more effectively than in India. If one could look back and see Japan, fifty years backwards, he would not find much difference between the intellectual, social, moral and religious ideals of Japan from those of India. The same is more or less true of the life of the masses in China.

Then there are other points of unity also. One is struck by the domestic life of the three nations being governed by the same ideals and the same sentiments. Why, in the matter of dress even, while there is a great deal of difference in the fashions and the outward look of the clothes worn by the three nations, there is yet a unity underlying the idea of dress throughout the Orient, similar to the unity in this matter which prevails in the Occident. The looseness of dress and the graceful flow of folds is the governing note of eastern dress. The ideas of decency in dress and appearance are practically the same throughout the Orient, and so different from the ideas which prevail in the Occident. Of course the climatic conditions have a great deal to do with that but we are not looking into the cause of these differences or similarities. We are simply concerned with the facts.

Mr. Dickinson finds many resemblances between Japan and ancient Greece, but he practically gives away the whole of his case when he says to the disparagement of the Japanese that the latter have originated nothing, that they took all their ideas from China, that their literature is curiously unintelligible and that their whole civilisation, though beautiful and passionate as it is, is thin and simple when compared with that of ancient Greece. It is damning with faint praise to say all this, and yet to hold that the foundation, so to speak, of Japan and ancient Greece is the same. Mr. Dickinson does not know that the Greek traits which he finds in the Japanese, *viz.*, that they are simple, subtle and passionate, quick to love, quick to quarrel, quick to die and kill, in everything intense and unreflective, are not confined to the Japanese alone in the East. The Sikhs in the Punjab, the Rajputs of Rajputana, the Maolis of Western India, the Nairs of Malabar, the Bengalis of East Bengal, the Burmese of Burma and Singhalees of Ceylon, not to say anything of the other nations of the East, of whom I have had no personal experience, are often credited with the same traits by their rulers, and more often than not, these traits are urged as valid grounds for refusing political privileges to them. It is said that these people are so quick in temper that they cannot be trusted with their own government. It is said that the masses of India are a set of undeveloped children, impressionable like wax and inflammable like straw, who are liable to fall at each others' throats on the smallest provocation. Of course I do not admit the accuracy of these estimates whether in the case of India or in that of Japan and China. Mr. Dickinson pays a just tribute to the chivalry of Japan and the code summed up in the term *"Bushido"*, but he evidently knows nothing of the chivalry of the Rajputs and the code summed up in the expressions *"Rajputi"* or *"Kshatrata"*. Why, you may as well take off some of the most brilliant pages from the history of *"Bushido"* chivalry in Japan and put them in the history of *Rajput Chivalry* and *vice versa*, without feeling that they are out of place in one or the other. A cursory study of Colonel Tod's Annals of Rajputana and Central India will show how much the life of pre-British India was dominated by what Mr. Dickinson calls chivalry and Bushido.

Mr. Dickinson shows a rather deplorable partiality when he talks of the Chinese being "a homogeneous people of the same stock, never conquered or traced, never affected in race, in manners, in laws and in language by conquest, never interrupted or disturbed for centuries in their traditional ideas and in their traditional manners of life." If this description of the Chinese is true, I am afraid, there is not much to choose between India and China. In stating the points of contrast between India and China Mr. Dickinson says :

"China has been and remains politically independent and united. This statement needs some qualifications but it is essentially true. The *Tartars* and the *Manchus* have conquered China but they have imposed on her nothing but a dynasty. They have adopted completely the manners, customs and ideas of the conquered. Of China it is truer even than of Greece that Capta ferum victorem cepit; not so India, the Mohammadans inspite of conversions remain Mohammadans, different in religion, different in sentiments, different in social institutions from the Hindus."

I am afraid Mr. Lowes Dickinson has been carried away by an unconscious imperial bias in making this contrast between India and China. When he talks of the Mohammadans of China he notices in them the manners, customs and ideas of the conquered. When he talks of the Mohammadans of India he only talks of the differences in religion, in sentiment and in social institutions. The fact is that the life of the bulk of Mohammadans living in villages in India is exactly the same as the life of the bulk of Mohammadans living in China. There may be some difference in the inhabitants of cities, and that is accounted for by the fact that India is closer to Arabia than China. On the Hindu population of India the

Mohammadan conquest imposed nothing but a dynasty or several dynasties. So here also the contrast fails.

Again Mr. Dickinson says :—"The various dialects of China, though unintelligible one to another, are varieties of the same language"—which is the case in India also, if the Dravidian Languages be excluded. *Sanskrit* and *Scripts* based upon *Sanskrit* have for ages provided a common medium of communication to the educated Hindus of all India. In fact I can go still further and say that Sanskrit has provided a common medium for the exchange of thoughts and ideas to the educated and religious-minded people of the whole East. In China as well as in Japan, in Ceylon, in Burma, in Indo-China it has been and is still a matter of pride for the educated people to know Sanskrit. The languages of these countries are full of Sanskrit words and their written books have a very large percentage of Sanskrit expressions. To know Sanskrit has been the badge of scholarship throughout the East at least ever since Buddhism was adopted in these countries. Sanskrit in the East has occupied and even now occupies the same position as Latin and Greek in Europe. This is another tie between the different countries of the East which binds them to each other more strongly perhaps than the points of difference noted by Mr. Dickinson. It should be noted that while Latin and Greek are more or less being deserted in Europe, the number of Japanese and possibly of Chinese too, who are taking to the study of Sanskrit is on the increase. The other day while travelling in the same boat with a Siamese gentleman, I asked him whether their language belonged to the Mongolian branch and was affiliated to Chinese. My fellow-traveller repudiated this suggestion as if that was a slur upon them, and said that their language was derived from Sanskrit, though the man seemed to be equally angry at my suggesting even remotely that they may have the same manners and customs as the Hindus.

What has struck Mr. Dickinson in the Chinese is, in his own language, "the secularism of the Chinese attitude to life." He thinks that mankind is the centre of the Chinese universe. Confucianism, adds he, may exactly be translated into terms of western positivism. It could not have been translated into terms of Hinduism. The fundamental mistake of Mr. Dickinson's view is in his conception of Hinduism.

Yet with strange inconsistency he admits that the religion of the masses of Chinese has always been superstition, whereas in India it appears to be true that the superstition symbolises spiritualism. That may be a compliment to the Hindus but it inflicts an injustice on the Chinese. Mr. Dickinson shows a deplorable ignorance of the deep currents of religion that have dominated Chinese life ever since the introduction of Buddhism. Japanese spiritualism is only a copy or an expansion of Chinese spiritualism. We find Mr. Dickinson making another mistake in considering ancestor worship to be rather a social than a religious institution in China, although he admits that it is the centre of the Chinese system. It is very difficult for the westerner to realise that in the East everywhere, whether in India, in China, in Japan or even in Arabia and Persia and the countries dominated by the Mohammadan religion, it is almost impossible to separate social life from religion. Everywhere in Asia, religion forms the fundamental basis of social life and that distinguishes it from the West. The East is dominated by the idea that life as a whole has one end, that it is indivisible, that it is organic and cannot be divided into water-tight compartments. The fundamental basis of life in the East is that the life of the body is only a part of a greater life, that it is a stage in the journey of the soul and that it should be used to the best advantage, to the evolution of that perfection which is the goal. No doubt sometimes emotional writers or superficial speakers are tempted to use language which tends to impress that life is illusionary and unreal. But by reading the whole context and following the arguments, one experiences no difficulty in finding that the unreality of life only means that this life is not the final be-end of existence. The East does not trouble itself with the supposition that man is or is not the centre of the universe. It is enough for the East to find that man occupies an exalted position in the universe and that his progress toward a more perfect being than he is at present, is the true goal of life. In that idea the whole East is united and therein distinguishable from the West.

The social outlook of the East is pervaded through and through by their religious outlook. The harmonizing of social life with religious ideals is the goal of all practical philosophy and the test of *real success* in evolving ideals and organizing life accordingly. The sacred books of the Hindus and the

Buddhists and also of the Mohammadans lay such an emphasis on this point that it cannot be ignored. That is why the social institutions of the East have, almost one and all, a religious basis. This is rather an evidence of their unity than otherwise. Then there is another very important point which unite the East, —their ideal of Womanhood. The present position of womanhood in the East is a discredit to it but in its essentials it is the same throughout the East. The women of China and Japan and Southern India have more of personal freedom, than their sisters in Arabia, Persia and Upper India, but the legal and social status of the women is practically the same throughout the East. Under Hindu and Mohammadan laws the legal status of women as mother, widow, daughter and sister has always been higher than in Christian countries. In the matter of personal freedom, and in the matter of choosing a mate the Eastern woman has been a victim of man-made social system in the East, but her position in these respects is practically the same throughout the East. The Eastern woman glorifies in her ideals of motherhood, of chastity, fidelity and unquestioned devotion to her husband and that is the common feature of social life in the East including the Semitic countries of Western Asia.

Coming to the art life of the East, that is a subject on which I am not competent to speak with authority. I do not know much of art. But there is an abundant evidence of competent people who have made a deep, in some cases a lifelong, study of Indian and Eastern art, which proves beyond doubt that here again there is a community of outlook, design, sentiment, inspiration and execution which unites the East. Before I proceed to quote the testimony of the Art experts, I would like to show what a strange view of Indian art, as distinguished from Chinese art, has been taken by Mr. Lowes Dickinson, who says on pp. 45-47 of his report as follows :

"This, which I call the secularism of the Chinese attitude to life, is also expressed in their art. *The art of India, in my judgment, has, as art, little or no value* (this, of course, is a highly controversial opinion), *but it is tremendously significant of the spiritual life of India.* It is all symbolic, and it is symbolic of those grandiose abstractions in which the Indian mind delights. It expresses an over-world of spiritual forces of which the world of sense is a shadowy and illusory manifestation. It does not interpret, it negates the ordinary life and the ordinary consciousness That is why it is so disquieting, so terrible, so monstrous to the Western spirit. But the art of China is through and through human. It is the kind of art that Romans, too, or Englishmen might have produced, if they had been gifted with æsthetic genius ; *the art of reasonable concrete-minded men, with a keen sensitiveness to the pathos and gaiety of human life, and the beauty and grandeur of nature.* It is characteristic of Chinese landscape-painting that it should include representation of the human observer. Their artists do not, it is true, treat nature as a mere background to human life, as, for example, the great Venetian artists do ; *but neither do they treat it as the vehicle of tremendous supernatural forces, which is the spirit of Indian art.* They treat it as a beautiful object, itself real, contemplated by a sane and sensitive human spirit. So with their poetry. It is cf all poetry I know the most human *and the least symbolic or romantic. It contemplates life just as it presents itself without any veil of ideas, any rhetoric or sentiment ;* it simply clears away the obstruction which habit has built up between us and the beauty of things, and leaves that, showing in its own nature, revealed but not recreated. Chinese art and Chinese poetry have the spirit of Wordsworth and of the most modern literary movement in French. Their art is a realism though not an actualism ; *a vision of what this life is as seen by those who can see it, not of some other world behind or above or outside it.*"

The italics are mine. Mr. Dickinson has not said much of Japanese art except by way of depreciation of the change in the ideals brought about by contact with the West.

Now let me give some quotations from the writings of western admirers of the art of Asia to compare with what has been said by Mr. Lowes Dickinson. On page 23 of his little book called "The Flight of the Dragon" (Wisdom of the East series) says Mr. Binyon :

"It is in the relation of man to nature that the painting of China and Japan has sought and found its most characteristic success. Probably the first thing that strikes every one on first making acquaintance with the painting of China and Japan, is the predominance of subjects taken from external nature, and the remarkably early period in which landscape themes appear. At first sight one might attribute this characteristic mainly to the passion for nature, adoration of flowers, which has for so many ages distinguished both the races."

"But it is something deeper than innocent delight which informs these schools of painting. Innocent and intense delight in the beauty of fresh blossoms is evident in numberless pictures of the earlier schools of Europe ; *but there these amenities of nature are but an episode.*"

"*It is a far different spirit which animates the Asian landscapes.* In these paintings we do not feel that the artist is portraying something external to himself, that he is caressing the happiness and soothing joy offered him in the pleasant places of the earth or even studying with wonder and delight the miraculous works of nature. But the winds of the air have become his desires, the clouds his wandering thoughts; the mountain peaks are his lovely aspirations, and the torrents his liberated energies. Flowers, opening their secret hearts to the light and trembling to the breeze's touch, seem to be unfolding the mystery of those institutions and emotions which are too deep or too shy for speech. *It is not man's earthly surrounding, tamed to his desires, that inspires the artist ; but the universe, in its wholeness and freedom has become his spiritual home.*"

"One might have thought that this identification of the life of man with the life of nature would have produced falsities of apprehension ; that human attributes would have been read into non-human existences. But no, it is European art that has done this. And why? For how many centuries, with us, was man regarded as lord of the earth, the centre of the universe, and the rest of nature as but existing to minister to his needs and his desires?"

"One might say that man has been a monarch, looking to his subject-world only for service and for flattery, and just because of this lordly attitude he has failed to understand that subject-world, and, even more, has failed to understand himself."

"This was the disillusion and dethronement which nineteenth-century science prepared for the proud spirit of the European man. But for the Chinese philosopher no such disillusionment could happen. He needed no discovery of science to enlighten him ; that enlightenment was part of his philosophy, his religion. He understood the continuity of the universe ; he recognised the kinship between his own life and the life of animals and birds and trees and plants. And so he approached all life with reverence, giving each existence its due value."

The reader would notice that in describing the difference between European and Asiatic points of view of art Mr. Binyon uses almost the same words which Mr. Lowes Dickinson has used in pointing out the difference between Western and Indian view point of life. Mr. Dickinson complains that "India has never put man in the centre of the Universe." (Page 11.) Mr. Binyon says the same of China and Japan. Then again speaking of the sources of inspiration of the Chinese and the Japanese art Mr. Binyon remarks :

"And so the sense of the impermanence of things, the transitoriness of life, which in Buddhism was allied to human sorrow, became a positive and glowing inspiration.

"The soul identified itself with the wind which bloweth where it listeth, with the cloud and the mist that melt away in rain, and are drawn up again into the air and this sovereign energy of the soul, fluid, penetrating, ever-changing, took form in the symbolic Dragon."

Speaking of Wordsworth Mr. Binyon points out that he is only "one of those isolated minds and personalities" in the west in whom an attitude corresponding to that of Asiatic artists is to be found, thus making him an exception. About the general attitude of Europe Mr. Binyon says :

"With all this world of ideas we are little familiar in Europe but the fascination and refreshment of this art is that it is inspired by ideas which are certainly not merely curious or of antiquarian interest, but modern, living, and of use to ourselves to-day."

Let us turn to another authority on Indian art, Mr. E. B. Havell, who has spent a whole life in the study of Indian art. In the first chapter of his book on "The Ideals of Indian Art," Mr. Havell quotes "the distinguished Japanese art critic," Mr. Okakura, as saying that "in the domain of *all art philosophy all Asia is one.*" Here is a direct refutation of Mr. Dickinson's theory. To this Mr. Havell adds :

"But if we apply western analytical methods to the exegetes of Asiatic aesthetics, we shall never form any just or complete conception of them until we have learnt to discard all our western academic prejudices and realised *the permanent importance of Indian philosophy and religion among the great creative forces which mould Asiatic art.*

"Again, it is only in the East that art still has a philosophy and still remains the great exponent of national faith and race traditions. In Indian idealism we shall find the key to the understanding, not only of *all Asiatic art,* but to that of the Christian art of the middle ages."

In his introduction Mr. Havell deplores the errors of western critics of Indian art in disregarding "the paramount importance of Indian idealism not only in Mogul art but in the great schools of China and Japan."

I could multiply quotations like these to any number, but I suppose the above are sufficient to establish (1) that Mr. Dickinson's dislike of Indian Art is not shared in by other equally or perhaps even more competent Art critics, (2) that there is a unity in all Eastern art which distinguishes it from the western and which Mr. Dickinson has in vain tried to demolish.

Let us now devote some space and thought to the economic life of the East. Mr. Lowes Dickinson admits that "like India, but unlike Western Europe, China is predominantly agricultural, and the bulk of her people are peasants. Like India, and unlike the West, indeed to a much greater degree than India, she is untouched by industrialism." This statement is as true of India and China, as of the rest of Asia except modern Japan. Before the advent of Europe in Asia the normal economic life of the continent was one of home or cottage industries, craft-organizations called Castes. Mohammadanism and Buddhism both do not recognize Caste as such but in either community one finds ample traces of classes or groups known by their occupations. The economic life of Asia is being dissolved by its impact with the West and in the interests of Asia the sooner it is shaped on European lines the better for it, from the material point of view. But the East would fain hesitate to incorporate European industrialism into its life. The force of circumstances leaves no choice. Refusal or delay means its continued exploitation by the West. Japan has already entered into the arena to the utter dismay of her European rivals. India would have done it even earlier than Japan and perhaps more completely, had it not been for the fact that her fiscal policy is being dictated from Whitehall. China is on the way to it and so are the smaller countries of Asia.

Thus it would be easily seen how the tests set down by Mr. Dickinson to prove the unity of the West, when applied to the East, establish the unity of the latter. But it was reserved for the present collosal conflict of arms which is desolating Europe, to establish conclusively that it was a mistake to suppose that the West was a unity. The Pro-Allies writers have now exhausted all the resources of intellect and ingenuity, of style and illustration, to prove that German "Kultur" and Teutonic spirit is entirely different from and inferior to the Anglo-Saxon as well as the Latin. Poor Mr. Dickinson, he could not possibly anticipate this.

A PATRIOTIC CHINESE LADY

By the courtesy of a young Indian lady I had the privilege of meeting a Chinese lady for the first time in my life, the other day. She is a student in one of the London colleges, and from her conversation it appeared that she was animated with the highest ideals of patriotism towards her country. Her ideas are so interesting and in some respects inspiring that I think they deserve a circulation in India, where I trust they will be read with great interest.

The first question that I put her was relating to the object of her visit to this country. She promptly replied, 'Study.' "Study, with what aim?" was the next question. "To serve my country," was the reply. She gave me to understand that she intended to consecrate her life to the service of her mother country, which, she said, was in a peculiarly difficult position just now. It required the fullest devotion and co-operation of all her sons and daughters to enable her to keep her head above waters and to preserve her independence. "We have enough of traitors," continued she, "but few who are imbued with lofty ideals for their country. My place is among my countrywomen and I intend to give my life for their service." But the depth of her patriotism was only disclosed when I questioned her about her religion. She is a convert to Christianity, while her parents are Buddhist. Inspite of her conversion to Christianity she is being maintained and educated by her parents. "What made you change your religion?" was my question. In reply she gave me three reasons. The first was that she wanted to lead the Chinese Christian women to Chinese nationalism. She was of opinion that Chinese Christians were lacking in a feeling of patriotism and it was necessary that they should have some ardent nationalists among them to lead them to the right path. The idea that underlay her answer was that Christianity had led them away from national ideals, and so it was necessary that some women who loved their country should work among them. The second reason was of a similar nature but of a general kind. She thought that for some time to come Christianity was bound to make progress in China and she would like the Chinese converts to Christianity to remain nationalists. "Both these reasons are secular," said I, "though lofty in one sense." "But I wanted a religion also," said she, "because in my opinion morality stands in danger without some sort of religion. And as the prevailing form of religion in my country did not satisfy me, I adopted Christianity." "But did you study your own religion?" was the next question I asked. "But we have no religion of our own," said she. "The teachings of Confucius are only general morality." "What about Buddhism?" said I. "Oh, it is a frightfully difficult religion for me," said she. "What is the chief merit of Christianity in your eyes?" asked I. "Hope" was the prompt reply. "Is indigenous religion in China altogether devoid of hope?" said I. "The prevailing customs in my country," said she, "make one extremely unhappy and hold forth no hope in any direction. Even Buddhism there has degenerated to gross forms of idolatry and formulæ." "How were you introduced to Christianity?" was my next question. "I used to read in a Mission School," said she.

"Do you believe in the infallibility of the Bible and in the virginity of the Mother of Christ?"

"I do not believe that every word of the Bible

is revealed, nor do I think it is necessary to believe in the virginity of Mary, for a belief in the sonship of Christ. Every one can be a Son of God."

"Your Christianity is hardly of an orthodox kind," said I, "and I think anybody can be a Christian of the kind without necessarily changing his religion."

The next question I asked her related to the women of China. She said, there was no purda in China, but the women were not allowed as much liberty as in England; for example it was rare for a Chinese girl to talk freely with a stranger even in the presence of her relatives and much less in their absence. The girls there, she said, generally marry at twenty; in better classes the bridegroom is only older by a year or two, otherwise there is no difference between the age of the parties to the marriage. "Is education common among the Chinese girls?" asked I. "Only so much as enables them to correspond," said she. "But they are now being educated highly and lots of them receive secondary education. Married life in China is not very happy, though there are very few examples of infidelity in married life."

"How do you like the English girls?" was my

next question. "They are very childish," said she. "It seems they have nothing serious about them; they care only about the pleasures of life." She proceeded to explain that was probably because their political domination in the world placed them in a position of ease. They have nothing to worry about, while we Asiatics are very anxious about our future and have to be serious about our present position.

"What about the Boxers rising?" "It was wrong," said she, "on their part to kill Europeans. We would have eventually won against Japan in the Chinese-Japanese war if our government had placed confidence in the people of China and had continued to fight. The Manchus, though they were not foreigners, were not strictly Chinese even."

"Do you like English dress, manners and customs?" asked I. She said, "I would observe them and dress myself in English fashion so long as I am in England, but I will revert to my own conditions of life when I go back to my own country, as I do not wish that my people should become denationalised by imitating others and losing their individuality. The Japanese also had at first completely adopted European manners, customs and dress but are going back to their own now."

"Do you think China will become Christian?" She said, she did not think so. Christianity will spread for some time to come, but will not be accepted universally. "Why are the Westerners so much afraid of the Chinese?" asked I. "Because they are very hard-working and industrious, and the white people cannot compete with them. Whenever they go to a new place they employ Chinese labour, but when the Chinaman begins to set up for himself they cry for his expulsion."

I may add that the young lady was exceedingly fair, pretty and intelligent. She spoke English fluently and gave indications of foreign accent only occasionally. My first acquaintance with a Chinese lady was very pleasant and exceedingly entertaining and interesting.

THE AMERICAN ECONOMISTS AND SOCIOLOGISTS IN ANNUAL MEETING

BY the courtesy of Professor Seligman of the Columbia University I was invited to attend the annual meetings of the American Economic, the American Sociological and the American Statistical Associations, held at Princeton, New Jersey, on the 28th to 31st December, 1914. Of these the American Statistical Association is the oldest and the American Sociological Association the youngest—this being the 76th annual meeting of the former and the ninth of the latter. The American Economic Association held its 27th annual meeting at the same time and place. Princeton, where the meetings were held, is a very small town, the head-quarters of the University of that name. The University has about 5000 students on its rolls and is perhaps one of the youngest American Universities, where the students prepare for the A. B. degree only and do not carry on any post-graduate studies. Yet it has splendid buildings and extensive grounds. The number of buildings included in the University is 84, the earliest having been built in 1765 A.D. Of these no less than 21 (perhaps more) are club houses or places for social gatherings. The buildings are beautiful and magnificent, fitted up with up-to-date improvements, sanitary or otherwise, lighted throughout with electricity and furnished profusely and superbly. The quadrangles afforded a beautiful sight when I reached there. Barring the paved footpaths and the temporary wooden track, all was white, spotlessly white. The snow that had fallen only two days before, was still lying in thick layers and had frozen. The high buildings with their tall towers and crowning minarets and domes made an inspiring impression. The town is a very quiet place—no factories and no markets. The surroundings are there purely academic and the atmosphere thoroughly non-industrial. The only other institution of note in the town is a seminary of theological learning where missionaries and ministers are trained for home and foreign service.

The three societies, the annual meetings of which I attended, are all allied. They deal with social questions of the greatest value to the nation and to humanity at large. In fact the addresses to which I listened with great attention left an impression on my mind that it was extremely hard to define their boundaries. They are so thoroughly inter-related and inter-dependent. Two of them have just at the present moment Presidents of Universities as their Presidents and the third is presided over by an eminent statistician. The American Economic Association has Mr. John H. Gray of the University of Minnesota as its President and the American Sociological Association, Mr. Edward A. Ross of the University of Wisconsin. The officers and members of the Executive Committees of these two are almost exclusively Professors of the different Universities in the U. S. A., and on the third also the Professors and officers of the Universities are in great strength. But it will be wrong to suppose that these Associations are purely academic. On the other hand they are thoroughly practical; in so far that every question is discussed in its practical application to the affairs of the U. S. A. What was most remarkable was that even the officers of the State took part in the debate and freely expressed their opinions and explained how the several questions under discussion were handled in actual administration.

Thus all sides of a question, purely academic, non-official, practical, and official were threshed out fully and every point of view was expressed, in good humour and without the least acerbity on either side. Sometimes pretty strong language was used by the critics of Governmental methods but it never transgressed the limits of good sense and was taken in good spirit. Here is an object-lesson for the Government of India. The idea of the "*purity of the academic atmosphere*" is at once absurd and unprecedented. There is no country on the face of the globe where teachers and professors do not take active interest in politics. To hold otherwise would be most injurious to the interests of good government as well as to the advance of scientific thought. Politics, Economics, Sociology and Statistics are sciences which cannot be separated from actual life. Theory and actualities act and react upon each other most wonderfully, in these departments of human knowledge. Professors are scientific experts who alone can correct the vagaries of high-handed and unprincipled officialdom; on the other hand, the practical administrative experience of officials and others engaged in business and the administration of the nations' affairs is the safest and the most effective check to the impracticability of mere theory divorced from life.

It is a most fatal mistake to cut off teachers and students from actual political life. Those who profess to teach political science, economics, and sociology, etc., by means of text books, without explaining their actual bearing on the affairs of the nation and the world and without throwing light on the actual phenomena which pass before the eyes of their students, are, to say the least, playing Hamlet without Hamlet. As a matter of fact, the European professors in India do not profess to perform this impossible feat. They can meet freely and speak adversely on the opinions held by the critics of the Government. That is in form. The embargo is on discussions in which the conduct of Government and the correctness of Government measures may be questioned. In our opinion this is a mischievous and short-sighted policy. A free and full discussion of the current problems in the class-rooms will be very useful even in the interests of law and order; many a wrong notion entertained by the students would be removed and the fallacies underlying them would be exposed. Fancy any University in England or in America rusticating a candidate for the degree of Ph. D. or Master of Arts, because when writing his thesis on Economics he criticises the current policy of the Government. In India this was actually done. The difference lay in the fact that the student concerned was not writing a thesis for the University degree but an exercise essay. The whole policy of the Government of India in this matter is impolitic, unacademic and unwise.

This was a digression. Now to revert to the American Associations referred to above. The first session was a combined meeting of all the three Associations. At 8 p.m. on the 28th of December the President of the University of Princeton welcomed the members in the name of the University and expressed the pleasure and the pride of the latter at their town having been selected for these annual meetings this year. He said the members of the Associations were philosophers in the strict sense of the term. They were concerned not only with what was, but also with what might be. Their investigations and labours helped in bettering and uplifting life and as such they were entitled to the gratitude of the nation in particular and of mankind in general. The speech did not occupy more than 20 minutes. After which the regular business of the session commenced.

First in order came the address of the President of the Economic Association, Mr. John H. Gray of the University of Minnesota. It was a written address, full of facts and able comments on the current economics and their relation to law. The burden of his remarks was the current idea of private property. He freely criticised the prevailing idea and practice and dwelt admirably on the problem of unequal and unfair distribution of wealth and comfort which resulted therefrom. He seemed to think, if I understood him rightly, that all private rights of property must be subject to the test of public welfare. He traced the growth of the current ideas of private property, beginning with individual competition and ending with the huge and gigantic corporations and trusts which were grinding and exploiting the community to the debasement of the individual worker. I am sorry that he read his paper very fast. The American pronunciation is also so different that it was at times difficult to follow him.

Next in order came the address of the President of the American Statistical Association. His burden was the lack of adequate attention both on the part of the Government and the public to the importance of correct statistics. He complained that statistics compiled by men who knew nothing of the science of Statistics and had received no training to qualify them for the task, could not be relied upon for the purposes of generalisation. He pointed out how the Government of the U. S. A. were neglecting this important branch of their duty and how unfavourably their action in this respect compared with that of Germany or even of England. He praised the German system and had a good word for the English also.

The third address was that of the President of the Sociological Association. He pointed out how the right of free communication including that of free assemblage and free speech was being violated by a combination of the capitalist with the autocrats in the administration and what a great danger to the progress of the community and the nation as a whole it constituted. All the four addresses, including that of the local President, did not take more than two hours and twenty minutes or perhaps even less. With the exception of the address of welcome, all the others were written addresses read by their respective authors.

The audience numbered about 400 and some people had come from great distances. In the United States distances are even greater than in India.

The next day the proceedings of the different Associations were held separately. I attended those of the Sociological Association. The proceedings began at 10 a.m., and lasted till about 12-25 p.m. The subject for discussion was "Free assemblage and reasonable restrictions on free assemblage." The first paper was read by Mr. Brooks. Without meaning any disrespect to the celebrated author, the speech seemed to be disjointed, I must say, yet the audience enjoyed it and listened to it with all attention. He was of course in favour of free assemblage subject only to considerations of common welfare. Next came a paper from the Commissioner of Police of the State of New York. He was not present in person as he had been prevented from coming by certain official duties, but his paper was read by one of his friends. While listening to his paper I thought what a blessing it would be to have such Commissioners in India. His theme was not to interfere with the right of free assemblage unless some overt act was done towards effecting a breach of the peace. He said the best way to keep peace was to let people have their say so long as they did not interfere with the rights of others, no matter what they wanted to say. He illustrated his ideas by actual facts from his experience as head of the New York Police. The third speaker pointed out the unsatisfactory nature of the law on the subject and elicited a great deal of laughter by quoting certain vague legislative definitions to be found in the codes of certain states. How I wished I had a copy of the Indian Seditious Meetings Act and the Indian Press Act and also of sections 108 to 110 of the Criminal Procedure Code of India to compare with the statutory provisions of which the speaker complained. This speaker was followed by the Commissioner of Police of Philadelphia State, and so the discussion went on until it was time to adjourn. In the afternoon session the subject for discussion was freedom of speech and in the next meeting on the following day, freedom of the Press and the freedom of education. In a few words I will try to explain the general position in the U. S. A. This country, as my readers know, is divided into some 54 states. All these states are independent of each other so far as their internal affairs are concerned. They can make their own laws in conformity with the

Federal Constitution and the original declaration of rights made at the time when America became independent of England. This declaration of rights allows the fullest possible freedom of speech, freedom of the Press and freedom of assemblage. Any law abridging that right is illegal and void. But freedom must be distinguished from license. Hence the necessity of some legislative provision to guard against license. But what are the legitimate boundaries of freedom and what is license? Herein views and opinions differ and have always differed and shall always differ. What is license to-day, becomes an approved doctrine and an accepted principle tomorrow. Vested interests, current opinions, prevailing notions of morality and theology, and last but not the least, the interests of rulers and principal classes, have always stood in the way of freedom of speech and freedom of assemblage. Yet the cause of freedom and progress has advanced and will advance, in spite of these restrictions and limitations. Europe has advanced on the corpses of hundreds and thousands of martyrs for the cause of freedom and has reached a stage where its people enjoy the largest possible freedom of speech and thought. The letter of the law means so little in the West. What is important is the spirit. But for this the prisons of Europe and America would be full of people who are the acknowledged leaders of society and states in these continents. All the same no one can deny that occasionally there are lapses from these normal conditions owing to powerful class interests influencing the judgments of those who rule, govern and judge. These give rise to complaints and agitation. American capitalists, financiers and wealthy men are just now very much exercised over the onslaughts of Socialism on private property. These people have great influence in the party organisations which really govern the country. They supply the sinews of war. The Socialists are comparatively poor. They make their voice heard by strikes, and the general block up of business. This conflict of interests between the classes and the masses brings about a clashing of forces. All the forces of intellect, and morality are on the side of the poor. All the forces of wealth, power, influence, habit and established religion are on the side of the capitalist. Hence the necessity of constant vigilance on the part of the former, lest the latter become too powerful and strong, and thus block the way to progress and reform. That is how the wheel of progress rolls on in the world and that explains the necessity of these interesting discussions, which the cream of intellectual America carried on in the meetings the proceedings of which I am reporting.

The Economic Association discussed the following subjects :

(1) Speculation on the Stock Exchanges and Public Regulation of the Exchange.

In India no one outside the circle of businessmen knows what is going on in these Stock Exchanges and what effect they have on the Commercial and Social morals of the nation.

(2) Market Distribution.

(3) The Relation of Education to Industrial Efficiency.

(4) The Effect of Inheritance and Income Taxes on the Distribution of Wealth.

The Statistical Association discussed :

(1) The relation of the Association to (*a*) Federal Statistical Bureaus, (*b*) State Statistical Bureaus, (c) Municipal Statistical Bureaus, (*d*) Public Service and Business Statistics and (c) Social Statistics and Surveys.

(2) Improvement and Extension of the Registration Services.

Besides this the Economic and Statistical Associations had a joint session wherein they discussed the Statistical work of the United States Government; and the Economic and the Sociological Association had a joint session to discuss the question of "The Public Regulation of Work."

When listening to these questions often the idea crossed my mind how many persons in India, outside the official circles, interested themselves in these questions and how many were qualified to take any intelligent interest in them and to what was the lack of interest and intelligence due. Of course there is only one reply. Firstly to the scanty provision made for the teaching of political and social sciences and secondly to the divorce of theory from practice and the bogey of the purity of the academic atmosphere. Why the men best qualified to stimulate interest in these questions, the professors and teachers of law, of economics, of political science, and of jurisprudence, are all muzzled. There is only one class that is left, *viz.*, the legal practitioners. The best of them are busy in making money and can spare no time for the creation and education of public opinion on matters which so vitally affect the prosperity of the nation and its intellectual, social and political progress. Hence the weakness of our political efforts and the ineffectiveness of our criticism of Government measures.
